M.L.
REA

FRIENDS OF ACPL

YO-AED-893

236.2 B47w
BIAMONTE, EDGAR, 1930-
WINDOW OF ETERNITY

**DO NOT REMOVE
CARDS FROM POCKET**

ALLEN COUNTY PUBLIC LIBRARY

FORT WAYNE, INDIANA 46802

You may return this book to any agency, branch, or bookmobile of the Allen County Public Library.

DEMCO

Window Of Eternity

by Edgar L. Biamonte

Ashley Books, Inc.
Port Washington, N. Y. 11050

WINDOW OF ETERNITY
(c)Copyright 1984 by Edgar Biamonte

Library of Congress Number: 83-9944
ISBN: 0-87949-230-9

ALL RIGHTS RESERVED

ASHLEY BOOKS, INC./*Publishers*
Port Washington, New York 11050

Printed in the United States of America
First Edition

9 8 7 6 5 4 3 2 1

All rights reserved, including the right to reproduce this book or portions thereof in any form or by any means, electronic or mechanical, including photocopying, recording, or by any information storage and retrieval system, without permission in writing from the publisher. All inquiries should be addressed to: ASHLEY BOOKS, INC., 30 Main Street, Port Washington, New York 11050.

Library of Congress Cataloging in Publication Data:

Biamonte, Edgar, 1930-
    Window of eternity.

    Includes bibliographical references.
    .1. Future life.   I. Title.
BL535.B47   1984   236'.2   83-9944
ISBN 0-87949-230-9

Table of Contents

Preface	vi
The Separation	11
Aspects of Consciousness	27
Love, Harmony and Perfection	45
Spiritual Existence	59
Religions and the Creator	71
Thought-sustained Dimensions of Existence	77
Dimensions of Hell	85
The Religion and General Consciousness of Group 2	95
Meditation	101
Visits from the Spirit World	111
The Power of the Subconscious	129
Purpose and Reincarnation	139
Bibliography	146

. . .those who have a closed mind will not get any evidence that will satisfy them.[1]

Seth

---

[1] Jane Roberts, *The Seth Material* (New Jersey: Prentice-Hall, 1970), p. 66.

2259938

To my wife, Antonie, with love.

Preface

Trying to prove that life continues after death is difficult for many reasons. Obviously no one has ever returned to describe the other world after being dead. Also, spirits are not clearly and openly communicating with us from the other world, despite man's many successes at seances and with other supposed mediums.

Yet at no other time has the public been deluged with so much information supporting the afterlife theory. Books abound on this subject. Tabloids and magazines continually report cases of people declared "clinically" dead for short periods of time who, miraculously revived by one means or another, then offer vivid descriptions about the world beyond. In the two years prior to writing this book, I watched three different television documentaries about psychic phenomena, all examining and tending to support the hereafter hypothesis.

Man's fear of physical death cannot be the only reason for our increased interest in this subject. Inquiring about death, we're probably tired of hearing the usual, stock replies: "You're going to heaven or hell," "You'll find out when you get there," "When you're dead, you're dead, so don't worry about it," and so on.

Certainly today's new and better means of reviving the so-called clinically dead have led to more reports than ever about people returning from the other side. Because of this, people are demanding explanations about what really happened to them when they were "temporarily" dead. Did they truly enter the next world momentarily, then return, or was their experience (assuming they experienced something quite unusual) some kind of illusion?

It is not my intention to condemn the general scientific world for not accepting the hereafter. Certainly, science wants documented, carefully controlled evidence — and therein lies the problem. Neither scientist nor layman can consistently and easily summon a spirit to discuss the other world. In fact, there is no hard evidence to support that we are truly capable of communicating with one of our best spirits, Christ, or vice versa, though we continually try and though many are convinced that we truly feel his spirit and love, if and when certain conditions are right.

Carefully controlled evidence is certainly highly desirable and truly necessary to prove anything conclusively. But since such proof of a hereafter might be impossible, we might only be able to theorize and speculate about it. Such speculation might be valuable in helping alleviate our general fears about physical death; it also might be closer to the truth than orthodox religion, philosophy, or anything else.

If life ceases completely after physical death, my energy writing this book (and your energy reading it) will have been wasted. On the other hand, if my speculations prove accurate, they could truly help us adjust more easily and quickly to a new, complicated dimension of existence that *seems* to follow physical death, even if we reject everything now.

Were I completely or even fifty percent certain that physical death were final, very little more would need to be said since such negative pronouncement describes its own finality. But I

Preface

believe in the hereafter for many reasons which will be discussed in this book, particularly because continuation is consistent and logical with many characteristics of the total arrangement of things.

Modern man, however, doesn't seem intellectually and emotionally prepared to accept the hereafter theory in the proper perspective for many reasons, even were he postively convinced of it. If the next world were scientifically proven to be generally peaceful, loving, and wonderful as claimed by many clinically "dead" patients who supposedly returned, probably more of us would justify suicide as an escape from this world's stress, evilness, and drudgery, even though some suicides who returned from the other side report receiving the impression that suicide is particularly condemned, since it is negative and contradicts life's force, especially physical life.

Advocates of our penal system might reevaluate their attitude if we suddenly discovered positively that capital punishment was sending convicted murders, for example, to a peaceful, loving world. In addition, if a better, happier existence were proven to follow death, some world leaders might feel more justified in waging war, arguing that the dead are ultimately going to be better off. In fact, anticipating a better afterlife could cause us to live particularly sensual, promiscuous, and materialistic lives on earth and even worsen our attitudes toward others!

At death, our complete physical life unfolds before us in the next world, according to many. Supposedly we feel the impact of our wrong doings and the hurt we might have caused others and ourselves while on earth. In addition, if the conscious is all that we retain afterwards, as many believe, the truly evil, unrepentant spirit will exist forever in a state of his own eternal grief or hell. The consequences of our evilness or goodness are apparently felt whether here or in the next world; therefore, perhaps proving the existence of a hereafter could truly motivate us into becoming more loving beings, even stimulate us into striving for moral perfection.

Of course, some maintain that keeping people guessing about the hereafter controls their behavior on earth. They claim that the more that people worry about "rotting or burning in hell," or the more they are fed superstitious, antiquated precepts about Satan, the better they will behave on earth. Such propaganda probably keeps these people in line, along with those individuals who lack the capacity to understand what being decent or morally good, truly is. But what about the rest? Shouldn't we attempt to enlighten for the benefit of the general good, rather than penalize many because we fear their possible evil behavior?

I support the hereafter theory not simply because it is positive but because of certain information, including some incidents in my life which I shall occasionally mention throughout this book.

Since certain matters cannot be tested or measured, or because they lie outside modern science, I cannot always document every statement I make. One of the purposes of this book, then, will be to make what I consider important connections and draw certain conclusions about various testimonies and information on the hereafter that others have offered, hopefully giving the reader new and challenging perspectives about both worlds.

Discussing the spirit world without relating it to how we think and operate in the physical world is imposible, since both worlds are connected. In fact, curiously, we ourselves embody both worlds, existing as part spiritual and part physical beings, though most of us hardly consider our spiritual aspects.

What might appear to be occasional digression thoughtout this book will only seem so because of the broad nature and scope of the subject matter. I have attempted to discuss many important aspects, ramifications, and especially characteristics about physical life, death, and the afterlife.

As a Westerner, I have tried to employ reason and logic — my heritage. But the concepts and ideas of this book were also written from and out of the deep inner self (or subconscious), in-

Preface

tuitively, as perhaps an Easterner might perceive physical and spiritual life. Therefore this book is something of a synthesis of both kinds of thinking.

Curiously, from the moment I began writing this book, I began to experience occasional spots before my eyes—tiny "bleeps" that in no way were connected to vision problems. They stopped afterwards and perhaps were the consequence of opening up new mental avenues of perception. On the other hand, spirits in the spirit world could have been responsible for them, attempting to signal or communicate with my spirit in the physical body. Electing to write about the spirit world, I might have somehow activated some different thought process which permits such communication, feeble and primitive as this was. This explanation might be more valid than the former, since the "bleeps" frequently occurred during languid moments when I wasn't taxing my mind. I mention this in the event that others might experience such sensations if and when they use their minds differently.

The book is also different because of repetition required by the unusual nature and scope of the topics. Such repetition was necessary because of what will undoubtedly loom as controversial conclusions I have drawn, perhaps controvesial only because of what we have been brainwashed or somehow led to believe, or learned on our own about life, death, and the afterlife. Clearly, it is impossible to view matters differently before a certain amount of "unlearning" has occured; or, phrased differently, sometimes the development of new attitudes and thinking requires some "unlearning." Or perhaps sometimes we aren't capable, willing, or ready to discard old ideas and concepts until or unless we repeatedly hear new and more precise ones.

Finally, to avoid confusion, I will always capitalize the pronoun *he* when referring to the antiquated concept of a single, male God ("He") and use lower case when referring to Christ ("he").

Chapter I

The Separation

Though psychics, parapsychologists and others have long known about the out-of-the-body experience, frequently called "separation," the general scientific world has not accepted it as a normal phenomenon occurring under even unusual conditions, nor is the average person generally familiar with it. However, it seems to be the key to unraveling the mystery about what happens after death.

In other words, if we can prove that some aspect of the self, soul, or consciousness can leave the body under certain circumstances, the question arises: where does it go if not into the next dimension — notably the spirit world.

Briefly, a separation is completely unlike daydreaming, dreaming, or sleep. It is also unlike hallucinating, the trance, or the hypnotic state. A separation is so unusual and different that those who experience it rarely forget it, while those who never did have trouble understanding it. It is so rare that most people will *never experience it in a lifetime,* much less perform it at will, although it might one day become as common as the hypnotic state. Nor would they perhaps want to, since it can be frightening, even if understood. But to say that a separation doesn't exist or is abnormal because it is rare is illogical. Birth and death are equally rare, occurring only once in a lifetime, yet no one would call either abnormal.

To understand the separation, try this experiment. Look up from this book and contemplate the wall or observe an object outside your window. Bearing in mind that your awareness or consciousness is somewhere in your head, consider the chosen object thoroughly and carefully for ten seconds or so. Now imagine your consciousness or awareness (your thinking ability) able to leave the body and proceed to the object, and from there, have the ability to see yourself just as clearly, vividly, and with the exact awareness as the object appeared from your reading location. In fact, you seem to possess most of the faculties that you had in the sitting position, when your consciousness was in the usual place, your head. You seem to perceive precisely how you perceived before, and possess the same intelligence and attitude. I say *seem* because not even those who have experienced the separation can categorically prove that the senses remain exactly the same. This is probably because we haven't been able to experiment or communicate with such "separated consciouses," to my knowledge.

What is most important is understanding and accepting as factual and valid the condition just described—that the consciousness can and does leave the body on certain occasions (the separation). Many people have described this experience and some can will it.

Dr. Raymond Moody, medical doctor, psychiatrist, and teacher of philosophy, was instrumental in stimulating new interest about what happens after death. Compiling information from many of his patients who "returned" after being reported

THE SEPARATION

"clinically" dead, he found many strikingly similar testimonies which he correlated in his book, *Life After Life*.[2] The book is extremely significant in describing many individuals who had separations during near-death experiences. The consciousness of those cited either returned to the body voluntarily or was "drawn back," or "pulled" after the heart and vital organs were revived.

Dr. Moody's book is particularly outstanding for being objective. He compiled and reported about 150 cases of separations that happened to near-death victims but didn't state his opinion or draw conclusions about them until the end of the book. Studying the many different accounts, the intelligent reader must certainly conclude that all these people couldn't be lying or in collusion. The interviews were apparently conducted separately, and each person was unaware of the other's experience. The many similar testimonies overwhelmingly support the theory that, although rare, separation is a valid phenomenon, a part of physical life and death.

True, Dr. Moody is honest enough to admit that, revived after having near-death experiences, some people *didn't* report anything resembling a separation, but several reasons might explain this. Such persons might have forgotten the experience, were too frightened to discuss it afterwards, or might have remained silent so others wouldn't consider them weird or even insane. Separation also might not have been triggered because the consciousness wasn't positive that final death was inevitable, strange as this might sound.

Analyzing his own cases, Dr. Moody concludes that the longer the near-death period, the stronger and deeper the separation. The shorter the near-death period the less chance of separation at all. For example, a person whose heart stops for a few minutes might not experience a separation at all, nor would

---

[2]Raymond A. Moody, Jr., M.D. *Life After Life* (New York: Bantam Books, Inc., 1976).

a person, necessarily, who wasn't completely convinced that impending separation spelled unequivocal death.

The point is that since many have reported separations, describing them quite similarly, we must logically conclude that the experience does occur under certain conditions. Testimonial evidence suggest many possible ways a separation might occur: (1) when one is pronounced dead (and is later revived) as from an illness, physical accident, or an attempted suicide; (2) when one is somehow convinced that death is imminent or unavoidable because of impending danger but is either mistaken or the danger is eliminated or avoided; (3) a separation might and can happen accidentally; (4) or as an extension of a dream; (5) or willfully, as many have testified like Robert Monroe, in his fascinating book about himself, *Journeys Out of the Body*.[3] Such individuals are frequently able to perceive verifiable information which they simply could not know unless they were "out-of-the-body."

The first type of separation might occur during a terminal illness. In most cases, the patient knows about his condition, and eventually the body reports the critical moment of impending death to the brain, or vice versa. How this is done is not entirely clear. Whatever, either the patient miraculously revives on his own or as a result of new, advanced resuscitation methods.

One can only speculate why some people do indeed revive while others don't. Perhaps either the body or brain, or both, somehow erroneously overestimates the body's deterioration or the situation, or has second thoughts, consistent with how we sometimes behave during physical life. Perhaps another part of the mind intercedes and *decides against final death* because of certain important purposes the particular consciousness (spirit) could only pursue in this particular body. The patient revives because of the doctor's efforts or a combination of all these

---

[3] Robert A. Monroe, *Journeys Out of the Body* (New York: Anchor Press, 1977).

THE SEPARATION

possibilities. He invariably describes the separation, and either asks for an explanation, which the world cannot offer, or remains silent.

I should explain here that I used *brain* instead of *consciousness* in the previous paragraphs not for variety but because the brain is analogous to a computor. Of course, considering a person's essence or totality, sometimes it is difficult to differentiate between the consciousness, the soul, the brain, one's awareness, and the self.

Considering the second type of separation, assume that a dangerous or fearful situation develops for a person. For example, he accidentally loses control of his car and drives off a steep cliff. Computing the situation, the brain (or consciousness) is convinced that death is imminent, although the brain might have somehow miscalculated the situation and be proven wrong. (Of course, precisely when separation might occur varies from individual to individual and depends on how he evaluates the situation and other variables such as if he is physically injured, how badly, or how sick, concerning the terminally ill.) In this case, separation might happen before the car crashes on the rocks below, the moment it does, or shortly thereafter. It might even occur if the impending danger were miraculously averted and the person survived, or it might not happen at all.

In whatever case, the consciousness must ultimately reenter the body or final death occurs. Once it does, such a person is usually puzzled. When he manages to describe the separation to others (if he does at all), they frequently attribute it to shock, hallucination, or temporary delirium, depending on the situation and those evaluating it. Incidentally, during separation, the person is frequently aware of hovering over and observing his own physical body at a distance, and, possessing instant mobility, among other unusual abilities, the consciousness eventually manages to join the body, sometimes after some effort.

WINDOW OF ETERNITY

The following example might help the reader further understand the second type of separation. Suppose a man finds himself standing before a firing squad, an extremely terrifying situation, convinced that death is unavoidable. Logically, separation should occur shortly after death by shooting. But if the man is extremely frightened, separation could happen even before his executioners raise their guns or give the count, and he could suddenly find himself hovering above, observing his physical body and the proceedings, while another aspect of his mind — probably the subconscious — keeps his body standing.

Perhaps another example of early separation is provided by those Buddhist monks who, protesting the Vietnam War, reportedly committed suicide by pouring gasoline over themselves, then setting themselves afire. Witnesses said they showed no signs of physical pain, suggesting that separation had already occurred. Protesting similarly, young Europeans, on the other hand, reportedly died amid great pain and agony, indicating no prior separation.

Concerning the doomed man, another possibility is that extreme fear could cause heart failure while he stood before the firing squad. In this case, the body would simply collapse and fall. Separation could occur at that precise moment or shortly afterwards, depending on the condition of his body, consciousness, and other variables. If no attempt were made to revive the body, he would most likely remain dead. If revival was attempted and was successful, the consciousness would somehow be drawn or pulled back, as discussed.

Supposing the doomed man was again so frightened that separation occurred while he was standing there, and then the danger was averted, i.e.; the order was somehow stopped or the executioners were somehow killed. Whatever, the consciousness would now have to reenter the body for it to become whole and to function normally. How the body would behave if the consciousness, still convinced of danger, decided against

The Separation

reentering for a while, would again probably depend on the particular mental and physical characteristics of this man. But the old clichés might describe his behavior.

He might simply stand there, stunned, begin walking around, dazed, or appear in what we call "a state of shock," as undoubtedly happened throughout history to soldiers convinced that the exploding bomb, grenade, or whatever should have killed them. He might need to be slapped or given a good shaking to "snap out of it." Though this sounds like a trite war film, slaps and shakes are comparable to modern efforts to revive a man, and probably had the same effect in somehow "pulling" the consciousness back into the body.

Considering another possibility, suppose the consciousness was so frightened that it refused to reenter the body at all. Again, the result would be a body without a consciousness, one run by another part of the mind, probably the subconscious. Without the consciousness, a person would ultimately be some kind of vegetable, probably behave insanely, appear in a continual state of shock. This would not be a coma, however, since comas are invariably caused by physical injuries, tumors, or strokes.

Separations, therefore, seem to follow a general pattern. They happen when the consciousness somehow leaves the physical body. Exactly when, how, and why frequently depend on the usual variables such as one's physical and mental attitude and awareness, and how one reacts to a particular situation. Just as no two humans are exactly alike, neither are separations.

I was closely involved in a separation of the second type. One day, years ago, my wife wasn't home and I was minding two of our four children. A sudden emergency arose. I had to leave the house immediately and had no alternative but to leave my four-year-old daughter in my five-year-old son's care. I recall hurriedly trying to explain why I had to go and assuring them that I would return quickly. Neither appeared too concerned, and I wasn't really worried because they were very well behaved and self-reliant, despite their ages, and the boy was already quite mature and responsible.

I left, confident of their safety. I returned soon after and was nevertheless relieved to find both where I had left them, my son playing on the floor and my daughter still on the couch flipping pages in a book. I asked if everything was all right, and both answered affirmatively, except that my daughter suddenly began describing very excitedly how she had been floating on the ceiling. I remember laughing, then explaining about the imagination. No one could float, I insisted with certainty, at that time unaware of separations. My daughter refused to change her story, no matter how I tried to convince her. Lest the situation became traumatic, I finally gave up, convinced that she has been fantasizing or hallucinating.

I recently discussed the incident with her, now a mature woman, and of course we both realize that she truly had had a separation (and has had similar experiences, since). She couldn't remember exactly why she had had a separation, and the answer could be locked in her subconscious. We concluded that she had probably triggered it out of some fear of danger to her, me, or both, or fear that I might never return. Though she had assured me before I left that she wouldn't be afraid "because she was a big girl," a phrase *I* probably forced upon her, perhaps I had unintentionally overdramatized the situation (because of my own fears and possible guilt about leaving them alone), and she actually became more frightened than both of us realized.

Whether she overreacted or lacked enough maturity to evaluate the situation properly is immaterial. She might have even feared death, although I'm not sure she understood death at that age. The point is that because of her mental attitude; because of her perception, awareness, or consciousness; or because of distortion of such, separation occurred.

It is interesting to speculate on why my dauther's consciousness did return to the body, since the same question can be asked in similar cases. If she were afraid of danger to herself, possibly it had second thoughts about staying out, as suggested before, and returned. Once outside the body, it might have clearly seen that she and her brother were not in any danger and rejoined the body. Perhaps she purposely triggered it because she knew, subconsciously, that by leaving her body she could get a better, overall view of the situation and be certain that danger wasn't lurking anywhere. Then, feeling more frightened outside her body, she reentered. Or, she might have been in conflict with herself, wanting to accompany her father on the one hand but also wishing to obey him on the other. Separation then occurred, *accidentally,* the consequence of trying to satisfy both urges.

Why the consciousness invariably returns, since many individuals reportedly find their new condition and existence superior to the old and quite pleasant once they overcome the initial shock, deserves consideration. (Some, of course, are not always entirely convinced that they are different until or unless they happen to see their body, or attempt to perform a certain physical task.)

For example, why return to a sick, decrepit body, as in the first type of spearation? Again, there are many possible reasons. As suggested in my daughter's case, many people might certainly be more frightened about finding themselves outside their bodies than facing the danger confronting them, so they some how manage to will themselves back inside. Others might have a strong desire to return, despite their physical impairment, because they know no other home, or because they still must live for certain subconscious reasons. They might return because they fear physical death, although terminally ill patients cannot always avert physical death just out of a strong desire to live, even though many such cases have been reported. Possibly many decide not to return and stay physically dead, which, of course, we never know about.

Accidental separation, suggested by my daughter's experience, is the third and perhaps the rarest type of separation, despite many reported cases. While teaching "Perspectives of Life and Death" at school, one of my students reported a typical, accidental separation. One morning his brother was lying awake in bed, perhaps in conflict with himself, as my daughter might have been. One part of himself urged him to rise and get ready for school, while the other part refused, wanting to remain in the nice warm bed. A separation apparently transpired in which the consciousness *did*, indeed, rise and leave the bed because the brother later described having become so frightened upon somehow noticing his body lying in bed that he rejoined it.

Separation of the fourth type seems to happen more frequently that most people think. The consciousness can leave the body during a dream. Many readers have undoubtedly had such clear, vivid dreams that they were convinced beyond doubt during the dream that they *weren't* dreaming and might have even told themselves so in the dream. Usually they awake soon after, stunned at realizing that they have been dreaming. But *were* they *just* dreaming? Perhaps they actually separated without realizing it.

Consider the following personal story. All my life I have intermittently dreamt about the house where I lived during my teen-age years, perhaps the most significant in one's life. One night, during a supposed dream, I saw myself sitting in the kitchen of this house, watching first one then another young girl, both total strangers, descend from upstairs. I told each not to be afraid of me. "This is an experiment," I conveyed without really seeing myself speak, common in dreams. They understood, assuring me they weren't afraid. The mother then appeared, another stranger, asked what I was doing there, and I replied similarly. But I immediately felt that she didn't appreciate my presence, so I somehow willed myself outdoors. Standing near the back steps, I felt particularly troubled, wondering how I was going to get back into my body. I recall noticing other people there, more strangers, especially a woman who somehow realized my dilemma or read my thoughts. She suddenly communicated to me that all I had to do was jump and take off, which I did. Seconds later, I felt myself swoop back into my body and I awoke.

Perhaps your immediate reaction is to label this a simple dream. Certainly that's all it might have been, even to a trained investigator, much less the ordinary layman. One could explain it as wishful thinking because consciously I'm somewhat reluctant to attempt a separation. So it occurs instead subconsciously, in a dream. Or, I might secretly wish to visit the old place but simply can't find time to make the long trip; therefore, I conjure dreams about the house. To some the dream might suggest a hidden desire to be young again, to relive and somehow change my teen-age years because they weren't joyous ones. The possibilities are numerous.

Dreams are unquestionably more complicated that most people realize. Aside from being manifestations of wishful thinking, events and places are frequently symbolic, incorporating bits of experience from the past, present and future, frequently in a mixed, disorganized, illogical order because they stem from the subconscious or inner self. They also mirror our conscious lives, reflecting various daily moods of happiness, anxiety, success, failure, depression, and so on.

Dreams embody frustrations, desires, and negative and positive aspects of ourselves, frequently fused and altered by sexual and other drives. Dreams can even be precognitive, visionary, telepathic, or clairvoyant. In fact, some who believe in reincarnation maintain that dreams are manipulated by old frustrations, desires, and experiences from former lives. In addition, others believe that we communicate with the subconsciouses of strangers in dreams (and I have had many dreams to support this theory), exchange mental notes, even transmit and receive certain kinds of energy from one another on earth and very possibly with those in the spirit world. Therefore, dreams simply cannot be interpreted quickly, easily, or positively, and I'm always awed by those in many different fields who can explain each and every one.

So I can only speculate about my dream. Upon close analysis, certain characteristics suggest that a separation might have occurred. For one, the dream was extremely vivid and in color, just as we perceive consciously. While I admit harboring a conscious desire to visit this house, the long trip and lack of time really aren't stopping me. In addition, telling the girls that I was conducting an experiment is almost like saying, "I'm not really dreaming," frequently a hint that the dream is more significant and meaningful than usual, possibly suggesting it's more than just a dream.

Everyone was a stranger in the dream, except me, of course, indicating that the two girls and mother might really live there. Interestingly, no close relative on either my wife's side or mine has two girls except my wife's sister whom we haven't visited in years. The preponderance of children in our families leans on the male side, with no set of parents having more than one girl, thus possibly ruling out that they were some manifestation of the family.

Certainly I could write to the current occupant at the house's address, explain what happened, and ask if two girls really lived there. The temptation is great, even though I'm sure the family might become alarmed, especially if they *do* have two daughters, wondering what kind of screwball this might be!

A stronger reason why I don't write is that the two girls might not belong to the present or even to this dimension. They could possibly belong to a past or future family. In other words, the dream could have been precognitive, capturing some aspect of the past or future. It is possible that I slipped into another

THE SEPARATION

dimension, notably the spirit world, where the three do indeed exist. Or the three could have been separated consciousnesses on a trip in the physical world where we all accidentally happened to meet.

Furthermore, accepting the possibility that my consciousness was really there and I communicated with three such people who truly exist in the physical present, I might have spoken with their subconsciouses and they might not be able to recall the incident consciously.

In *Journeys Out of the Body,* Robert Monroe discusses many incredible personal experiences during his "willed separations," the fifth type. One of his many extraordinary experiences is particularly significant in substantiating that consciousness, or some aspect of the mind, does indeed separate. On one occasion during separation, he "talked" to a woman in the physical world, urging her not to forget their conversation. The woman promised she wouldn't, but to make sure, Mr. Monroe pinched her just about the hips.

Later, back in his body in the physical world, Monroe questioned her about the incident. She admitted not remembering their conversation (implying that it had been made with her subconscious, as in my own case with the girls and mother), but definitely recalled the pinch, which she described as almost causing her to "jump a foot." Thinking her brother-in-law had been responsible, she relates having turned around, surprised to find no one there. As proof, she showed Mr. Monroe the red mark just above the hips.[4]

Unless all this is exaggeration or lies, which I disbelieve until or unless proven, especially since many of Monroe's experiences were performed under controlled situations, this is incredible information. It not only seems to substantiate the separation

---

[4]Monroe, pp. 55-57.

theory but begs acceptance that the consciousness does have power out of the body.

Considering my dream again, I could have somehow projected a ghostlike image of myself into the house, in which case a mother and two daughters, if existing in our present, might still be trying to recover from the shock. But I reject this explanation because accidental and/or willful projections or materializations of the self are very rare. Besides, none of the three appeared frightened at seeing me sitting at their kitchen table.

What happened outside is a different matter. Since it is highly unlikely that a crowd of physical people was truly there, I don't believe that I communicated with subconscious minds, as might have happened in the house. Accepting that some part of me was truly there, whom did I then communicate with? Once again, the simple answer could be no one, since this was just an ordinary dream.

Another theory is that I simply communicated with some aspect of my own mind, perhaps the subconscious. The most fascinating interpretation, however, is that I contacted consciousnesses existing outside their bodies and/or spirits, or energies from another dimension, notably the spirit world, and one of them helped me return to my body. Mr. Monroe's book is full of such excursions and communications. In fact his separations are so much more definite and far-reaching that my incident seems almost comparatively inconsequential. I certainly recommend his book for analysis of "willed" separations.

The most convincing part of my dream is the difficulty I had getting back into the body, frequently typical of initial out-of-body experiences. True, I knew about separations before this dream so admittedly I might have merely fantasized the difficulty in the dream. But the feeling of "swooping" back into the body close to the moment of awakening did not seem like part of the dream or like anything that I had read about concerning reentering the body after separation. Something seemingly unusual had happened, as though I had really reunited with the body from some "trip," typical of many returns to the body described in Mr. Monroe's book, which I didn't read until months after this dream.

Critics of the separation theory claim that the consciousness might not really leave the body. Information might simply be "picked up," clairvoyantly or telepathically. But this ability to perceive beyond the senses is invariably lost after near-death patients are revived, indicating that the information was obtained during separation. Let me note here that there is a great difference between someone like Kreskin reading telepathically or "seeing into things" and gathering information during willful separations or even during near-death situations. Most mentalists like Kreskin deny that separation occurs during their telephathic or clairvoyant acts.

Confronted with today's enormous testimonial evidence, I had no other choice but to accept the separation as a valid human experience, although I considered it quite incredible and unusual when I first heard about it and still do.[5] But because something is unusual, new, unproven, different, or hardly investigated doesn't invalidate it.

Throughout history, man has struggled and even risked his life attempting to uncover or explain the unknown in order to eliminate his inherent fear of it. The problem with accepting the separation is not just simply fear of accepting something new and different, but having to deal with the tremendous implications and the vast areas of new unknowns that such acceptance undoubtedly reveals.

---

[5]Carlos Castenada, author of *The Teachings of Don Juan* and other similar books, had many similar out-of-the body experiences, induced naturally or by drugs. Jane Roberts, author of *The Seth Material* and similar fascinating books has willfully separated frequently.

Chapter II

Aspects of Consciousness

Hopefully, the reader now accepts the separation as a normal, human function which everyone can trigger under certain circumstances. Now we must evaluate various testimonial evidence concerning what exactly transpires during the separation process.

According to many of Dr. Moody's cases, individuals generally hear themselves pronounced dead, followed by an unusual "noise, a loud ringing or buzzing,"[6] which, generally, seems to be the sound the consciousness makes leaving the body. Precisely why and how it does this, or whether or not this is just a mental aberration or the only way the mind can compute this experience is hard to determine, but this sound is inaudible to others. In addition, not every near-death patient seems to hear the same sound. Some have heard music,[7] others,

---
[6]Moody, p. 21.
[7]Ibid., p. 30.

nothing. Again, what one does or doesn't hear seems to depend on individual differences, possibly how long one is declared clinically dead and/or the depth of the experience. But invalidating the separation because of these dissimilarities would be like rejecting dreaming as a normal human function just because people experience dissimilar dreams.

After being revived, most of Dr. Moody's clinically dead patients reported having moved through a long, dark tunnel or cave. Again, the tunnel or cave (if, indeed, it is either) is hard to explain, although perhaps the movement of the consciousness out of the body is somehow mentally computed this way. Mr. Monroe frequently hears a hissing during separations but doesn't mention the tunnel effect. Remember though that his are *willed* separations, unquestionably different from those experienced by near-death patients. Some part of his brain, perhaps the subconscious, controls his body functions while his conscious self is gone. Concerning similarities during separation, Dr. Moody's patients and Mr. Monroe are all capable of hovering above and "seeing" their bodies clearly.

Another important difference between Mr. Monroe's and Dr. Moody's separations is that, depending on the experience's depth, most of Dr. Moody's patients are confronted by what he calls "a loving, warm spirit. . .a being of light"[8] which somehow nonverbally requests the patient to evaluate his life. The patient then somehow sees a replay of the major events of his life. Mr. Monroe never mentions the light or the panoramic playback, and probably doesn't experience such phenomena because his brain knows that his body isn't experiencing a physical death situation. Nor does he encounter the being of light or anything like it. This might be because the being of light "understands" that Mr. Monroe is not dead yet and therefore has no need to evaluate his life.

---

[8]Ibid., p. 58-59.

Aspects of Consciousness

Certainly if I accept the separation theory suggested by Dr. Moody's patients, Mr. Monroe, and many others, it would be illogical to deny the being of light merely because it sounds more fantastic than the separation.

The question arises, does the conscious summon the being of light or does this light come voluntarily, somehow aware that a conscious has left its supposed dead physical body and now exists in its own domain? In addition, can we conclude that the being of light is capable of erring if the conscious is ultimately pulled back into the body, following successful revival efforts? Or, equally possible, does the being of light know the person will be revived and purposely appears for some reason? (Some of Dr. Moody's near-death patients who were revived imply that having experienced the being of light made them more spiritual, tolerant, and loving.)

Such questions are difficult because we can only speculate on the answers, but speculation is perhaps vital, considering the dramatic nature of this information. Because of religious indoctrination, many of Dr. Moody's patients equated the being of light with God, Jesus, or a guardian angel, any of which are also possible. But since most nonreligious people generally did not make such an analogy, the idea seems subjective, possibly even wishful thinking.

If we consider the being of light a spirit in the spirit world, like one of us after physical death, only far more developed, on a higher moral level and far more loving, we can answer the questions previously posed. The being of light *does* seem to greet those reaching the spirit world, even if they are pulled back into their bodies. Clearly, the being of light might have no way of knowing who will remain in the spirit world and who will be drawn back following a near-death experience.

Revived near-death patients report that the being of light

glows with a magnificent, almost indescribably bright light.[9] Interestingly, in *Paradise Lost,* the seventeenth century English poet, John Milton, seemed to be on the right track in describing angels, comparable to the being of light, as possessing a "transcendent brightness,"[10] while Satan and his crew, portrayed as having rebelled from heaven, lack such luster and will eventually glow progressively less and less. True, this is an imaginative interpretation of the Bible; yet, this conception seems to spring from the inner self, the apparent bridge between ourselves and the spirit world. Many of Dr. Moody's patients report observing "a realm of bewildered spirits," comparable to purgatory, who also appear quite dull.[11]

I doubt if the being of light is God because, generally speaking, I don't believe that humans are capable or perhaps even worthy of direct communication with God. In fact, since God hasn't appeared before any of the great, loving, moral people in the past or present (except occasionally, according to the Bible whose information is highly speculative, relative, imprecise, and controversial) why should He come before our spirits after physical death? A more complicated arrangement than suggested by the Bible seems to exist.

Ministers and other readers might consider such talk blasphemous, and perhaps are recalling such clichés as: "God moves in mysterious ways," and that if God doesn't manifest Himself before a particular person, that person is unworthy of God. (If the latter is true, God has consistently chosen not to ap-

---

[9] Using Ruth Montgomery as a medium, Arthur Ford, speaking from the other side, also claims that souls "shine with varying degrees of light." See Ruth Montgomery, *A World Beyond* (New York: Coward, McCann and Geoghegan, 1971), p. 67.

[10] James Holly Hanford, ed., *The Poems of John Milton* (New York: The Ronald Press Company, 1953), p. 208.

[11] Raymond Moody, Jr., M.D. Reflections on *Life After Life* (New York: Bantam Books, Inc., 1978), p. 18.

pear before *any* man throughout history.) Whatever, there is no tangible proof, much less scientifically controlled, documented evidence supporting the belief that morally good people frequently receive God's or Jesus' energy or spirit, although this is certainly possible. In fact, I not only like to believe this, but actually do, although I express it differently.

Conceivably, God might possibly tune in when important, unselfish requests are made, like prayers for peace or to end suffering, or possibly only out of curiosity to see how we are developing or how many of us have truly arrived at this or any other level of consciousness (awareness). Emotionally, I would like to believe He answers us and positively interferes in our lives. Intellectually, I know He doesn't. Why should He, when He knows that we are as much responsible for and capable of solving our problems as we were for creating them?

In fact, God demonstrating His power or displeasure by miraculously stopping any particular war in history, for example, would have undoubtedly failed to end all wars or make us love or fear Him any more or less. Even had God done so, and man could agree that He had, which I seriously doubt, man would probably have soon forgotten, denied, or misinterpreted such intervention. Depending on its nature, such dramatic interference might possibly have momentarily frightened us but not forcibly changed our attitude about war or suddenly made us all good or loving unless we were emotionally ready for such change.

Trying to understand God's ways, get into His mind, or understand Him is certainly difficult, if not indeed arrogant. Certainly it presupposes that one has approached or is even on the same level with a supreme being responsible for creating and setting in motion not only the material world, including vast, incomprehensible, almost infinite energies stored in countless galaxies throughout the universe, but also all the dimensions of existence comprising the spirit world whose combined energies amount to more than man can conceive, much less compute. Thus, though one can only speculate about God, I am convinced that the being of light isn't God because the human consciousness seems far too simple, if not base, to receive the enormous power or love energy which we attribute to our concept of a single God. Receiving the full impact of such a force would undoubtedly blow man's mind.

On the other hand, if trying to understand God's mind is arrogance on our part, then man has been so guilty since history's beginning. In fact, some religions not only believe that God is completely knowable but that the Bible, which they claim was written by certain prophets supposedly inspired by Him, is capable of answering questions about Him, man, and the nature of the physical and spirit world which is not only highly improbable but simply untrue. In additon, arguing that the Bible is the ultimate truth simply because its authors were supposedly God-inspired is invalid, since we could say the same about every morally great author and book. I accept that certain forces (or even a single force) might have influenced and/or inspired the prophets, but what these forces were (and still are) and whether or not God was responsible and exactly what God is are all different and highly controversial matters. Certainly no single book (including this one) like the Bible can lay claim to possessing all the answers about God and man.

Let us consider how the Bible probably developed. Throughout history, men have struggled to enslave others or make them follow certain laws. Practically every nation has done this up to and including modern times.

The Romans during Christ's time exemplified this development, conquering neighbors as well as those people across the seas, imposing their laws and lifestyle on the conquered. Although the Jews were thus enslaved, they were still convinced that God favored them. They were probably no more morally better or worse than the Romans, but rather simply victims of their time and environment.

Because they suffered from enslavement, persecution, and injustice, they created the Bible out of a deep, subconscious need to believe and hope in something more just. As Christianity began to spread, new world leaders adopted the same Bible to reinforce their desires, even against their own followers if it were expedient, until differentiating between the persecutors and the persecuted became difficult.

Persecution has been and still is a way of life, despite the Bible and frequently because of it. Just as before, today's leaders still can justify war, when killing contradicts the sixth commandment and similar moral concepts. They can still justify attending church and supposedly following their religion on the one hand while praying for God's help to destroy the so-called enemy on the other. The masses not only support such contradictions but are invariably convinced that congregating and muttering certain words in a particular manmade structure called a church will "save" them, exonerate their sins after physical death, permitting entry into a special, glorious domain called heaven.

Considering this paradox, the point is that man cannot force, frighten or punish others into being good, since force or punishment immediately negates goodness.

Men have wept about man's plight, his frequent evilness, unpredictability, corruption, and have prayed for God's help. Men have longed for and dreamt about a better world, have tried to create utopias, all doomed from the start because man's consciousness had not and still hasn't progressed to a level that can permit and sustain such a world. We keep looking for help from beyond ourselves (from our God) when, clearly, we have been left to help ourselves — which we have the potential of doing.

Embodying the consciousness of their times, the Jews of old became inspired, had dreams, saw visions, foretold the future, probably had ESP, and ultimately became what we call "the prophets," authors of the Bible. Many of us revere these men like gods. Religions and beliefs have been molded around them. But did God inspire, communicate with the prophets of the Bible, or give them spiritual energy? Perhaps indirectly, and once again depending on what we mean by God, although possibly they might have gathered strength from themselves, even possibly from the spirit world. Or perhaps they absorbed strength and energy from others on earth.

Consider an example of consciousness from modern times. Persecuted, enslaved, and having suffered for centuries, the blacks needed a leader, one who could somehow lift them out of their misery and help them gain equality and justice. Blacks probably weren't forever verbalizing this need, although many certainly did. But verbalization wasn't necessary. Their conscious yearnings for equality, justice, and freedom drifted into their subconsciousnesses and dreams. Consciously, many wept, prayed, and hoped for positive change, until out of that world of consciousness emerged Dr. Martin Luther King. Again, was God responsible for sending King to the blacks? Some believe He was, and since we are all connected with God, how can we disagree?

Considered differently (perhaps more realistically), the consciousness of the American black was so shaped and developed over the years that unless conditions radically improved and/or changed, a man like King would inevitably one day be born out of black yearnings (Christ having possibly also been born out of similar deep yearnings). Or, considered still differently, it was inevitable that a spirit would probably choose to reincarnate in a particular family and the situation would ultimately be right for that spirit to pursue a particular purpose because of prevailing conditions.

True, the black consciousness also possessed a hateful, vengeful, militant side (as many blocks of consciousness do) which demanded violent action against the whites and almost took complete control of the black movement. Why the nonviolent faction headed by King ultimately prevailed was probably less a matter of luck than most people think, since our problems, situations and environments are created out of or as a result of the prevailing consciousness. Possibly thought power from enough consciouses desiring a solution through peaceful means managed to endure and overcome those demanding the same through force.

Attributing the nonviolent solution to God's interference in man's affairs presents the same problem as before — of determining what God is and trying to justify why He chose to intervene then rather than at a graver, more horrifying moment in man's history. And I'm still not ruling out that spiritual power from the spirit world might have helped or inspired the entire nonviolent black movement, including King.

The Bible is a reflection of man's consciousness at the time it was written. The Bible was needed, so man wrote it for his own emotional and intellectual protection. Emotionally he needed it to give him hope and soothe his suffering; intellectually he accepted it because he lacked the scientific knowledge and the sophisticated modern mind to challenge it. It has long since become almost obsolete. It has stimulated false hope about heaven and God, and unnecessary fears about hell and the devil, the latter probably nonexistent or certainly not as the Bible has portrayed. Individuals revived from near-death describe a more precise, different afterlife which the Bible hardly details. In addition, because the Bible frequently contradicts science, it has probably caused more anxiety, fear and confusion than it is worth, particularly today. It is also frequently negative, generally unloving, and contains considerable violence, particularly in the Old Testament.

True, when all else failed, the Bible's teachings held many families together and still do. Were it not for the Bible, many people would have probably gone berserk struggling to live under various tyrants and trying to endure periods of great misery and suffering throughout the ages. On the other hand, the Bible has been indirectly responsible for stimulating many wars throughout history, and contains many vivid descriptions of battle, which God supposedly inspired.[12] If we continue maintaining that the Bible is God's word, then God looms quite illogical—one who apparently had enough love to create us but who contradicts the sixth commandment by inspiring his own creations to kill off the so-called evil ones, also his creations. I cannot accept the Bible's conception of God because He was formulated and conceived out of a consciousness that has long since outlived its times.

If one refuses to accept such reasoning, insisting that this particular God-concept created and frequently inspires men like Christ and King, why did He somehow fail with Hitler and similar tyrants throughout history? The devil influenced such evil men, some people quickly point out. They would also like us to believe that according to the Bible, God not only was stupid enough to create the devil but was (is) even dumber to allow him to exist.

---

[12]Genesis 18:26-32. God implies that He would destroy a city if it contained ungodly inhabitants. Genesis 19:24-26. God rains down fire and flaming tar from heaven, destroying Sodom and Gomorrah and other cities. Genesis 35:4. God takes sides, imbuing His terror on cities, so they won't attack Jacob as he journeys through with his household and family. Exodus 14:24-27. Observing the Egyptians, Jehovah begins harrassing them, removing chariot wheels. The lord finally drowns them at sea. Numbers 10:9. Moses only needs to sound his trumpets, and God will save him from his enemies. Numbers 21:2-3. The lord helps the people of Isreal defeat the Canaanites. Numbers 31. Following the lord's orders, Moses destroys the Midianites for leading the Israelis into idolatry. Deuteronomy 7:16-20. The lord urges the Israelis to destroy all nations and offers his help, also 20:16 and 31:4-6. Joshua 6:17-23. The lord orders the Israelis to destroy the city of Jericho and even helps, crumbling the walls. Joshua 10:8-10. The lord threw the enemy into a panic, so the army of Israel could slaughter great numbers, also 11:6-9. Samuel 15:2. God's commandment is for Saul to destroy the entire Amalek nation. Kings 20:13. Speaking through a prophet, the lord supports King Ahab's battle against king Ben-hadad of Syria, and in Kings 20:28, promises to help him defeat a vast Syrian army. Ephesians 6:10-14. God advises his followers to wear his armor and wage war against the evil rulers of the world whom Satan supposedly controls.

Of course, God promises to annihilate him and his horde some day. Why God has made man wait and suffer so long is hard to accept until we hear the fairy tale about a couple called Adam and Eve. Clearly, another system of things is in operation, and the greatest sacrilege and blasphemy is to blame God for man's own immorality and evilness, which many of us refuse to accept because our enormous egos, arrogance, and selfishness blind us.

Because of its importance, let us continue explaining the idea of mass consciousness, using Hitler as an example. Because Germany was defeated and lost territory in World War I, many Germans felt humiliated, cheated, angry, inadequate, and wanted revenge. The Depression exacerbated their frustrations and misery, creating an attitude which filtered into their dreams and seeped into their subconsciouses. Had Germany's consciousness been different, the German people probably would not have permitted a man like Hitler to come to power. Hitler was clearly born out of the consciousness of his times.

In fact, most Germans were stirred by Hitler's early speeches (before he came to power), blaming the communists and Jews for Germany's troubles. Many either believed him or were simply indifferent, the latter being just as accountable for his rise to power. Not only did he ultimately renege on his promise to act lawfully after Hindenburg named him head of government, but he quickly eliminated individual rights and created the Gestapo, which ruthlessly hunted down, shot, or jailed anyone suspected of opposing him. By the time Germans comprehended him, it was too late.

Many of Hitler's top officials such as Goebbels, Himmler, and Goering were probably psychotics, reflecting not only Hitler's particular consciousness but society's and even the world's. Mankind is as much to blame for Hitler's existence as various civilizations are for leaders like Stalin, Amin, or Nixon, or for the common mugger on the street and the slums and ghettos that disfigure the world's cities. The consciousness of Jim Jones developed out of the prejudiced, unloving American consciousness. If the Guyana tragedy or something similar wasn't inevitable, it was possible because of this consciousness.

Considering what television portrays and what the general public reads, perhaps the yardstick for measuring what the masses have become, Western civilization buys and accepts considerable violence and cheap morality. Perhaps only when the world's consciousness progresses to the point where we refuse to be so shaped (or misshaped) and demand more meaningful subject matter or ways to improve and develop our consciouses, will constructive change and improvement begin.

Apparently man's consciousness after World War I was such that secret treaties were overlooked (the London Treaty of 1915), and the victors simply demanded the spoils, a superb example of shortsightedness, greed, and lack of compassion.[13] Colonies were indiscriminately removed from Germany and provinces from Turkey, and it was not truly within man's general consciousness to settle all colonial claims justly. Peace followed, but because it was not born out of man's true forgiveness, reconciliation, and love for one another, a second world war was inevitable.

World War II erupted for many reasons other than smouldering resentment over how World War I was settled. The nature of man's overall consciousness was chiefly responsible. Basically, war springs from man's deep, perhaps innate feelings of greed, ambition, selfishness, jealousy, mistrust, and so on, and unless these attitudes are somehow permanently replaced by true love and compassion for one another, wars and other evils, even including diseases, will always exist.

Consciousness is so important that another illustration might

---

[13]"World War I", *The World Book Encyclopedia,* 1974, xxi, 378.

ASPECTS OF CONSCIOUSNESS

be necessary to fully explain. All individual families, for example, possess their own particular kind of consciousness — general attitude and awareness — with no two family consciouses alike. Most families are quite average, neither overly moral nor immoral. Comprising most of civilization, this group is the general masses, and the largest, which I will call group one. Such families frequently practice some form of bigotry or prejudice, and occasionally lie because they have difficulty keeping promises or following certain rules, or for other reasons. They are mostly selfish and greedy and usually need some reward, motive, or incentive to be reliable and predictable. They rarely disobey existing laws, mostly because they have been brainwashed into believing that these laws are unquestionably right and fear suffering the consequences if they get caught disobeying them. Most of those from group one lack a sense of morality built on truth, justice, and unselfish love for one another.

They generally have love for immediate family members and relatives, some friends, and occasionally neighbors, but frequently little or none for those of different religions or for people whose parents might have been born in a different area from theirs, sometimes even if only a short distance away, or for those who are decidedly different from them.

They are frequently capable of giving unselfishly to their immediate family but secretly expect or would like in return some remuneration, reciprocation in some form, if only respect, loyalty or cooperation, especially from relatives and friends. Rarely do they give freely of themselves or materially, particularly to strangers. Generally, they tend to exhibit jealousy towards whomever possesses more material wealth, education, or a better position in life.

Their meager concept of justice is mainly altered by their emotions, which continually cause considerable anxiety toward others and themselves. They are very concerned with physical appearances and hardly consider spiritual matters, much less know or care about the soul.

Despite living in a fairly sophisticated, scientific world, many from this group follow very antiquated religions, worshipping in certain elaborate structures on particular days and requiring males rather than females (for very illogical reasons) to help them pray. These males consider themselves God's spokesmen; worse, many people pray to crosses and idols, contradicting the laws of their own Bible, or follow ritualistic practices that have no worthwhile meaning.

Most members of group one generally fear death and are secretly convinced that despite their so-called sins they are definitely going to some region called heaven. Most don't know where this is, and have been so involved with the physical world over the centuries that they hardly contemplate this region or are afraid to, lest they discover it doesn't exist or that they truly possess the qualifications to enter a place called hell, which they have created in their own imaginations to frighten themselves into being good.

In addition, this same group has the usual apprehensions about everything: from concern over their material goods to fear of losing their jobs or becoming sick. They love socializing, particularly belonging to organizations, and devote considerable time and energy toward some or all of such organizations' goals, frequently at the expense of other far more important responsibilities such as becoming involved with and raising their children properly. They like believing in causes (rarely considering their morality or justice) and blindly follow so-called leaders who rarely possess any vision or imagination for constructive change but who simply follow past precepts and morality, frequently unjust and evil. They secretly reject or suspect all people who don't belong to the same organization, cause, or religion as they.

Obsessed with physical longevity, they indirectly pay scientists to determine what foods or environmental conditions harm the body, then proceed to eat those very foods or continue the same lifestyles, rationalizing that they only live once.

Members of this group are capable of and/or possess much hate, particularly the young males who are always willing to don a uniform and fight whomever their government tells them is the enemy, even though so-called enemies and friends sometimes change within a decade, depending on leaders, political climate and other variables. They kill mostly for what they see as patriotism or glory, or because of reverence for an inanimate piece of cloth supposedly symbolizing where they were born, now live, what language they speak, or who their forefathers were and what they did or didn't do, although many simply enjoy the adventure, excitement, and the money received for such services. Many such individuals argue that their government forces them to kill when, realistically, the jails couldn't begin to hold even a small percentage of them if they organized and refused to fight.

So-called leaders are mostly chosen from group one. They run the affairs of the geographical area where their group lives. Because these leaders generally possess a conscious similar to that of their group, they usually rule poorly and harbor the usual anxieties. Truly great moral people accidentally rising to power (extremely rarely) are frequently so unlike the group that they are quickly removed politically or by assassination.

Parts of the world yielding more natural resources than others are greatly desired, causing leaders of such lands to charge exorbitantly for what they accidentally happen to "own," to cling selfishly to such resources, and/or to blackmail other nations who desperately need what they have. This causes the usual jealousy, hatred, and sometimes war.

A single world government could probably eliminate such problems, along with considerable disorganization, disharmony, and dissatisfaction. The League of Nations attempted to do just that but failed because of haggling, hate, suspicion, and anxiety. Our present U.N. has little chance of becoming an effective governing body unless and until all nations are ready to relinquish all their governing power to it. Besides, those from group one would probably have to possess an unselfish, loving consciousness before nations would be ready to relinquish or share their excess wealth. Lacking the proper consciousness throughout the world, this group is simply too emotionally and intellectually unstable to accept the logic of a single world government, much less set it into motion.

Many from this group recognize such faults, problems, and their own inadequacies but have successfully rationalized them, refusing to change them or themselves, mostly because others don't, they argue, so the cycle continues. Others from this group are simply ignorant of such matters or don't care what they are or what effect their actions have on others, as long as they can "do their own thing," which is mostly selfish. Because this large group maintains many of these attitudes, the overall world consciousness hardly changes.

The second group of people possesses a baser, more immoral form of consciousness. Group one categorizes them as "the misfits of society," and they include criminals, the insane, drug addicts, alcoholics, fanatics, and others—actually group one's byproducts which they hardly recognize or conveniently refuse to.

Hitler is a good example of someone from group two. Ironically, had he not been surrounded by those from group one, he might never have become a ruthless dictator. Similarly, had Jim Jones lived in a loving society instead of a prejudiced one, he probably wouldn't have wanted to build a utopia in Guyana, nor would anyone have needed to believe in or follow him. Furthermore, had Jim Jones not been born, someone else would have probably attempted a similar movement to compensate for what his environment (comprising group one) is and is not because of the nature of its consciousness.

The third group comprises highly moral people, unquestionably existing on civilization's periphery. These individuals invariably dedicate most or all of their lives and energies towards others' benefit and well-being without expecting reward or payment. They are emotionally and intellectually mature enough to realize that helping others and making them happy contribute to their own joy and happiness, payment enough. Jesus undoubtedly heads this nonviolent, loving group, along with people like Buddha, Schweitzer, Gandhi, King, Einstein and others.

Such individuals hardly desire fame, power, or material wealth. They are capable of giving much of themselves, unselfishly, not only to their families and relatives, but to others, even strangers. They are generally honest, loving, just, truthful, and happy, realizing that such qualities are logical since goodness attracts and enhances goodness, while evilness, attracts the opposite.

Certainly many of those from the other groups frequently take advantage of these people. Sometimes they sense being so exploited, sometimes not. But this is usually almost immaterial since they thrive on their own goodness, although they are not immune to suffering from such evil. They are most appreciated and particularly loved by those in this and the spirit world who have attained a similar level of consciousness or who simply recognize them for what they are.

Such highly moral people hardly need to attend church, rarely do, and usually dislike those (frequently their morally inferior counterparts) who attempt to frighten them into being good. Already good, they hardly need laws to force them to be so. Their goodness stems from within, a spiritual morality, usually harmonious with most existing moral laws, although these people invariably follow their own consciences. Frequently more spiritual and more truly religious than most churchgoers, such people are often misunderstood or viewed suspiciously by those from other groups.

Nor do these truly good people really need to pray in the conventional sense. Their thoughts and actions are so moral and loving that their entire being reflects a state of reverence and prayer. They love all creatures, from insects to man, whatever his level of consciousness, because they generally accept and respect the supreme conscious's creation of life. They realize that destroying human life is negative, meaningless, and contradictory, and that those who, throughout history, killed humans to satisfy their leaders' wishes were unfortunate victims — pawns — of their times. They recognize that even killing lowly life forms is frequently immoral except, perhaps, in rare, life-threatening situations.

For these highly moral people to associate or make friends with individuals who are selfish, who advocate war, violence, or racism, or possess other unloving, immoral qualities is frequently difficult, if not impossible. Certainly they try to change such people, and they might ultimately accept their friendship if they change. If they don't reform, these highly moral people probably avoid them out of self-preservation since they cannot flourish lovingly and happily if they are forced to be with those of a base, immoral conscious. Lacking the same earthly ties and obligations with one another once we enter the spirit world, we probably exist and communicate mostly with those possessing similar and/or compatible consciouses.

Only if and when those from group one and two can somehow develop a sincere, loving consciousness will the world truly change and *peace truly prevail*. Whether this is simply wishful thinking, is immaterial. The point is that the overall world consciousness can only become loving if and when individual consciouses do so. Are individuals moving in this direction? If they are, the movement is progressing far too slowly and perhaps did not start soon enough to avoid our own annihilation.

Chapter III

Love, Harmony, and Perfection

George Ritchie was a serviceman who became gravely sick and landed in an Army hospital in 1943. Convinced that his train was leaving without him (he was supposed to embark on the Army's doctor-training program), he reportedly bolted upright in bed, left his room, and raced down the hospital corridor, practically bumping into an orderly who didn't notice him.

Once outside, Ritchie assumed he was running, yet had a strange feeling that he was flying, a thought which he of course pushed out of his mind. Recalling that the orderly hadn't seen him, he paused near a telephone pole to collect himself. He reached for a guy wire and was staggered when his hand went through it. Realizing something was wrong, he dashed back into the hospital and eventually found his body, although only after some difficulty because the bodies looked similar, and he didn't know he had experienced a separation.

Wondering how to enter his body, he was further amazed when the room suddenly filled with an unusually brilliant light, unquestionably the very "being of light" Dr. Moody's patients described. Ritchie immediately equated the light with Christ and love, and the room was "flooded, pierced and illuminated, by the most total compassion" Ritchie ever experienced.[14]

In the being of light's presence, Ritchie saw a panoramic playback of his life. Ritchie was then given an opportunity to look at what he calls "spiritual worlds," as Weiss explains. One in particular contained sculptors, philosophers, composers, and inventors, great libraries and scientific laboratories. Another contained a city constructed out of light "in which the walls, houses, and streets seemed to give off light, while moving among them were beings as blindingly bright as the One who stood beside me."[15]

Ritchie was revived after being declared dead from double lobar pneumonia for at least nine minutes. His experience parallels in many ways cases cited in the Moody books. For example, Ritchie, as Moody's patients, was confronted with an extremely bright light. This "being of light" triggered a replay of the patient's life and asked what the patient had accomplished. And, like Moody's patients, Ritchie suffered no brain damage from his experience.[16]

Notice also how Richie's experience substantiates my claim that during separation the consciousness apparently perceives as though it were in the body, until or unless it performs some particular physical task that signals otherwise. Once outside his body, Ritchie hardly realized any change in himself until he reached the guy wire, for example.

That Ritchie (now a doctor) and Dr. Moody's patients could have accidentally imagined similar experiences seems almost impossible. Certainly Mr. Weiss and Dr. Moody could be exag-

---

[14]Jess E. Weiss, *The Vestibule* (New York: Ashley Books, Inc., 1972), p. 65.
[15]Ibid., p. 67.
[16]Ibid., p. 65.

Love, Harmony, and Perfection

gerating or lying, or could have somehow collaborated. But I doubt it. We could continue disputing this information when, in effect, it begs acceptance for what it is, testimonial evidence supporting the strong possibility for dimensions of existence *beyond physical life.*

As mentioned earlier, many of Dr. Moody's patients consider the so-called being of light Christ, God, or a guardian angel. For months I tried to determine which of these it might be, along with Dr. Richie's light. And then the answer hit me. Most followers of a particular religion saw the light as some subjective manifestation of their religious training, particularly Christ or God, whereas near-death patients who didn't follow any particular religion did not, implying that the being is something or someone else. (If it is Christ or God, we can only wonder how either could appear simulatneously to the daily dying multitude throughout the world.)

Either Christ or God has the power of doing anything and/or everything, many might argue. True enough and certainly possible, but there is a simpler explanation. The beings of light are simply individual spirits (like you or me but certainly more developed or possessing a more advanced or loving consciousness) who have chosen to appear before us shortly after physical death as some kind of guardian, possibly to ease the shock and help us make the transition into the spirit world. Glowing with indescribably loving brilliance, they are undoubtedly great spirits who probably reincarnated many times in order to attain their levels of awareness. Dr. Ritchie saw entire cities of such spirits, supporting the idea that the being of light is one of many advanced spirits, not Christ.

One aspect that most near-death survivors describe is the feeling of love surrounding the being of light. Indeed, love cannot be underestimated. In fact, from what they have learned about the spirit world, Dr. Moody's near-death patients (and many similar cases others have described) generally agree that our two main pursuits on earth should be to love one another and acquire knowledge, in that order.[17] The love idea is particularly significant. God probably created the universe out of a strong, loving desire to create something beautiful and perfect. And the universe *does* work perfectly, despite man's stress-filled nature and frequent violence which contradict that loving force or nature.

It appears that the joy, love, and peace which all of Dr. Moody's near-death patients claimed they felt in the next world support the idea that a feeling of love probably pervades the spirit world, perhaps motivated God into creating the physical world, and is the stuff that holds all dimensions together.[18] If true, love's importance cannot be underemphasized, and, considering civilization's general unloving, stress-filled characteristics, man seems out of harmony with all the dimensions of existence, including the physical world.

True, so many of us have adjusted or hardened to this difficult, seemingly complicated world that we don't even realize how much mental and physical punishment we have endured until we are temporarily released during a near-death experience, or when the end finally occurs. Some might have adjusted or accepted stress and mental pain so completely that they hardly ever stop to consider them. One day, to prove that most of us seemingly suffer much mental pain, I asked my students how many had suffered or were still suffering mental pain, and I was somewhat surprised at the number of hands, practically the entire class.

These were young adults who hadn't really begun to enter the so-called real, adult world. Unless they somehow avoid stress-

---

[17]Moody, p. 65.

[18]Revived near-death patients, spirits like Arthur Ford and others, repeat this love idea continuously. See Moody, *Reflections on Life After Life,* p. 96; Moody, *Life After Life,* p. 92-93; Montgomery, p. 29.

filled jobs and relationships and somehow relieve their stress, suffering, or anxiety through some kind of therapy, consultation, exercise, meditation or somehow simply learn to be loving beings, they will probably break down in some way or experience the unual unhappiness in our civilization.

Interestingly, none of the revived patients who experienced love and warmth from the being of light reportedly considered, much less attempted, reciprocating in kind, indicating what unloving people we generally are. In fact, in our society and other capitalistic countries, loving people generally loom quite strange, particularly to city dwellers where life is frequently hectic, businesslike, and materialistic.

We're all aware of the new fears and anxieties in the cities because of increased crime which our false sense of values and material greed have helped stimulate. Instead of placing such a high value on wealth (intentional or not) which attracts some havenots to risk everything (sometimes even physical life) to attain, we should deemphasize material things and make a serious attempt to see that the havenots are provided for.

To put it simply, peace and harmony will only return to the cities, if not the world, if and when we're really prepared to help and sacrifice for the poor and needy, not just talk about their plight or initiate ineffective or token reform to help them.

Our meager conception of love is truly weird. A fond hand rested on the shoulder of a person of similar sex, for example, is usually misconstrued as homosexuality, particularly in America. We have so many hangups concerning the opposite sex that showing genuine concern—love and compassion for one another for long durations—is frequently interpreted as an invitation to bed by either sex. Consequently, depending on our motives, we find ourselves continually behaving cautiously or role playing with the opposite sex, and rarely do we really openly and freely give of ourselves to one another.

So a disparity exists between the spirit world's apparently

peaceful, loving nature and the physical world's lack thereof. Before discussing the implications of this gap in the next chapter, analyzing the apparent nature of the spirit world is necessary, particularly considering its close relationship to the physical world.

To being with, lacking a body, we will not generally experience physical pain in the spirit world unless we are somehow mentally convinced we should. Those finding themselves in the next dimension after separation testify that they can pass through physical objects on earth such as walls and buildings without difficulty.

But apparently our physical world is as much the wrong domain for spirits as the spirit world is for us, explaining why trips to either side are rare and difficult. For example, after separating from the body the consciousness exists in spirit form, operates in another dimension, and lacks the ability to communicate with us except perhaps subconsciously, nor can it manipulate objects in our physical world, except very rarely.

Outside their bodies, Dr. Moody's near-death patients report struggling but failing to communicate with their doctors, nurses, and others in the physical world but report the ability to pass through objects. The consciousness in the spirit world also seems capable of stimultaneous communication with more than one spirit, compared to one at a time in the physical body. The consciousness also seems to possess other unusual characteristics such as thought mobility, also to be discussed in the next chapter.

In *Journeys Out of the Body,* Robert Monroe describes several levels or dimensions of existence he perceived in the spirit world during his "willed" separations. He calls one such existence Locale II, which he considers closest to our material world, Locale I, possibly even pervading it without our knowledge. We cannot normally perceive this dimension because it lies outside our usual senses and is hardly recognizable, much less proven by science. But such matters shouldn't negate its possible existence. Man would hardly have discovered or invented very much had he always been deterred every time his senses or science failed to tap into the unknown. We have difficulty perceiving differently because we are taught from infancy to use and respond to the five senses. Not taught from infancy to communicate telepathically, mentally move objects, or see various energies and forces lurking about the physical world, we generally reject such abilities and/or forces.

In Carlos Castaneda's remarkable books about Don Juan's teachings, Don Juan continually warns (teaches) Carlos to be alert for unusual stimuli lying outside or beyond his usual senses. Interestingly, only after adjusting his perception (chemically or naturally) does Carlos eventually perceive some incredible entities and forces (stimuli) beyond the physical world, which Don Juan has perceived all along. Apparently such adjustment enables Robert Monroe to "see" into his Locale II. In fact, possibly Castaneda, Don Juan, Monroe and many others have shared similar perceptions of some aspect of the same dimension or dimensions without realizing it.

That Don Juan and Carlos might be hallucinating or imagining everything is certainly possible. But discounting such unknowns simply because the senses cannot perceive them is illogical, especially considering the many different perceptions of people possessing ESP. The outsider simply might not be tuned in to compute such different stimuli, for example; or, closing the mind to their possibility, he might block out whatever mentality or kind of consciousness is needed for such perception.

Considering the various types of perception, body control, and other phenomenon achieved under hypnosis and through posthypnotic suggestion, implies the mind's awesome, untapped potentialities. But forcing the mind to work harder or at least perceive differently or accept new concepts is another matter.

I lived in the country when I wrote this book. One night I happened to look outside and was amazed to see a seemingly soft, cottony substance float past, close to the window. It wasn't a meteor, car or plane lights, nor had I been drinking because I don't drink, and I don't have vision problems. It was unlike anything I had ever seen in my life and haven't seen anything like it since, but perhaps *experienced* is a better word since *seeing* usually implies only sight. I didn't have time to call my wife, who was in the next room, and by the time I reached the window, it was gone.

It could have been anything, including a UFO, although unless my perception had somehow been distorted, it seemed too small. It could also have been some aspect of another dimension, possibly some manifestation of energy or intelligence from Locale II or another reality. Whether or not my wife would or could have seen it might not have proven or negated its existence since she might not have been perceptually capable of perceiving it.

To illustrate the last point, consider the following incident. One night my wife asked me to hammer a nail into the wall because she wanted to hang a painting we had recently purchased. After getting the hammer, I prepared to tap the wall for a solid sound, saying I didn't want to ruin the wall. Suddenly she interrupted me, stunned with surprise. Somehow she was able to see the studs through the wall! As hard as I tried, all I could see was a bare, cream-painted wall. Realizing she wasn't joking, I asked her to point out a stud where she wanted the picture. She did, I nailed, and there was the stud. But this clairvoyant ability left almost as quickly as it came, nor could she repeat this feat after the picture was hung nor ever since. Her particular mental or emotional attitude at the time — perhaps concern that I might damage the sheet rock wall searching for the stud — might have initiated it.

On another occasion, while we were sitting on our deck intermittently discussing life after death, my wife saw an extraordinary, distant flash of light. I didn't see it because I had been reading and might not have been capable of seeing it at that moment. It was unlike anything she had ever seen, and it didn't appear like lightning, especially since the day was bright and sunny and thunder didn't follow. It could have been her imagination or the power of suggestion because of our discussion. Again, it also could have been some aspect of another reality which somehow momentarily altered her mind or consciousness or somehow made either capable of tuning in to it. Or she simply might have been "ready" to experience such a stimulus.

Incidentally, the fact that she might have imagined it neither minimizes the incident's significance or its perception. That we hear a siren in the physical world, for example, doesn't make such external stimuli any more valid, realistic, or superior to the perceiver than purely internal or imaginative stimuli, especially considering that people possessing ESP perceive differently. In addition, all stimuli affect the consciousness anyway. Of course, in order to function and communicate properly with one another, we're forced as physical people to perceive in "the proper perspective," or like most everyone else. The point is that sometimes differentiating between outer or inner stimuli is difficult if not immaterial in instances like this since the brain or other internal receptors compute both, and such information or experiences are invariably stored in the subconscious.

Does discussing such unknowns, keeping one's mind open or alert to them, actually open the mind or consciousness or make either more receptive to different and unusual stimuli? This is certainly a possibility, but how or why might be difficult to determine and depend on such variables as one's emotional attitude at the time and certainly individual differences. Our minds and perceptions are constantly changing and developing, especially because all of us have the potential for some kind of ESP, whether scientifically accepted or not.

Consider how we invariably respond to illness, particularly in Western civilization. The first symptom sends us running to a doctor for a diagnosis. If the first opinion is shocking or dissatisfies us, we seek more opinions until some consensus is reached and we're finally resigned to accepting the illness in the usual civilized way, unconditionally. Such an attitude tends to reinforce and possibly even stimulate illness, mentally and physically, into our system.

Suppose we feel sick, and our doctor tells us we have the flu. Hearing such news from a doctor, whom we generally respect, we begin behaving predictably, especially if we already feel terrible. The disease having been substantiated, we now can sniffle, sneeze, and cough more significantly. We complain more to others about how sick and miserable we feel and possibly receive some sympathy and pity. We sometimes lose our appetites, lose weight, and begin viewing the world more negatively than usual.

Long since conditioned *against* mentally helping ourselves, accepting other's mental help, or allowing the body's natural defenses to work, we accept chemical treatment. We usually assimilate aspirins, cough syrup, and various antibiotics as well as the usual bad food. One can only speculate how many diseases have been incorrectly diagnosed or unintentionally suggested, then supposedly cured by unneeded medicine.

Considering how society has conditioned us for so long, I'm not suggesting that in our present state of development and consciousness we can suddenly turn on a mental switch and will away disease. We would have to make many important changes in our lifestyles before we could even begin to do this or prevent disease from occurring in the first place.

Chemical treatment does work most of the time, but mainly because Western society has persuaded itself to believe that it works better than, say a witch doctor's antics; yet witch doctors have been known to cure diseases and without harmful side effects. The point is that because of what we have become, we have locked ourselves into believing a certain way about diseases and their cures when, in fact, we have the potential to completely eliminate disease if and when we sufficiently and properly alter our consciouses.[19]

Surrounded by a generally unloving society, no wonder we get sick and have difficulty curing ourselves. Conversely, we probably wouldn't become physically and mentally sick so often or at all if all of us were truly loving. If someone accidentally did get sick in such an environment, mass love or love energy could conceivably cure him. Faith healers probably cure by combining positive thinking and the power of suggestion with an ability, conscious or not, to tap into and use such energy. While some faith healers successfully help others without renumeration, others demand payment for an ability that appears to be inherent in all of us. Still others are simply quacks or swindlers, or insist that Jesus and/or God has given only them such powers.

The following personal story exemplifies the power of love and the different types of perception. One night my daughter, who was living in Arizona, telephoned the terrible news that she had contracted cancer. At first my wife and I were stunned. Recovering from the initial shock, we decided to alter our thinking. We decided to reject the doctor's diagnosis in order not to mentally reinforce it. Crying or bemoaning her condition surely couldn't help, we reasoned, nor would discussing the disease or connecting her with it.

Despite our emotions, which we simply had to control for her sake, we had to think positively, an old philosophy, and somehow will her to get well. We resolved to think only loving,

---

[19]Speaking through Jane Roberts, the spirit Seth comments that, "Illness is often the result of dissociated and inhibited emotions" and cautions against the danger of accepting illness as a part of the self. See Roberts, pp. 30 and 168.

positive thoughts about her, and alerted others in our immediate family to follow suit. We also convinced her not to brood or feel depressed. Because of the family's general consciousness about such matters, she too had already changed her attitude after also recovering from the news. She seemed quite receptive about our suggestion to keep occupied, think positively and happily, and feel confident about rallying mental and physical forces to overcome the disease.

I decided to try and send her some love energy, or possibly alert some energy, spiritual force, or whatever power we might be capable of tapping to overcome her illness. The next morning after meditating (which I had been doing twice daily for years), I pictured her vividly, then "willed" her entire body with all the love and energy I could muster for several minutes. I told no one about my experiment. Two nights later, my daughter called and related the following without my prompting.

"You know, Ma and Dad, something very strange happened to me toward morning a few days ago (corresponding exactly to our time difference). While lying in bed, I remember awakening from a pleasant dream. Suddenly some strange force held my head immovable, and I suddenly felt a fantastic warmth, like energy, spreading throughout my body. It was a wonderful, beautiful feeling, and I felt completely invigorated after it left. It made me feel very happy, rejuvenated, and I thanked it.

Needless to say, my wife and daughter were amazed when I told them what I had attempted or believed I had accomplished and my daughter's apparent reception of whatever I had managed to enlist and/or send.

We're all familiar with the power of positive thinking but not in connection with such forces and surging energy. Of course, although she did recover, I can not say for sure that this experience aided or even cured her. And yet, how can I or anyone else *be entirely sure it did not?*

Attempting to explain the incident, perhaps all we can do for now is generalize until more research is done in such areas. But somehow, someway, the proper conditions were present for the incident to occur—because of her, me, or the family's combined efforts or consciouses. Whether or not this energy exists on earth or in Monroe's Locale II, III, the spirit world, or is from another spiritual dimension, or the result of well-directed mental energy, or was truly from God or Christ, or a combination of these, is hard to say and probably immaterial.

In his book, *The Crack in the Cosmic Egg,* Joseph Pearce suggests the reinforcement theory which he calls "the circularity of expectancy verification, the mirroring of reality of a passionate or basic fear."[20] Having contracted cancer, his wife seemed to follow the many instances of cancer that occured in the family. Fear of contracting the disease probably pervaded the consciouses of this entire family. Undoubtedly, cancer had been discussed repeatedly, reverberating in their subconsciouses and probably even emerging in their dreams, reason enough for the disease to snowball, although other factors such as diet, heredity, and environment might have played a part. Perhaps the disease will run its course if and when this family becomes so accustomed to its occurrence that they hardly discuss or think about it.

---

[20] Joseph Chilton Pearce, *The Crack in the Cosmic Egg* (New York: Pocket Books, 1973), p. 8.

Chapter IV

Spiritual Existence

Because of the differences in dimensions of existence, spirits have as much difficulty communicating with us or functioning in the physical world as we have contacting them or functioning in their world. Ghosts are as rare in the physical world as people like Robert Monroe operating in the spirit world. Talking ghosts are equally rare, although chanting, whisperings, and related sounds supposedly produced by ghosts (more accurately referred to as trapped spirits on earth) have been reportedly taped on ordinary tape recorders.

Despite unusual incidents and various claims, spirits and ghosts also lack the necessary power to move objects in the physical world and cause bodily harm or have difficulty doing so. Communicating with us is also difficult for them because they lack a physical body and the necessary vocal apparatus for speaking; therefore, they need a living, physical body or some other vehicle (like a ouija board) through which to contact us.

There have been so many cases of spirits entering and speaking through a living person's body (called a medium) while that person is in a trance that this is almost common knowledge.

One particularly incredible "take-over" of the body happened to Jane Roberts. Using the ouija board with her husband on several occasions, Mrs. Roberts suddenly became aware that she was anticipating her husband's questions directed to the board before he asked them. As these sessions continued, on one occasion Jane Roberts (her pen name) fell into a trance. Her body was "taken over" by a spirit from another dimension. Eventually, during one of these sessions, Mrs. Roberts's voice changed, became more masculine, and the spirit ultimately identified himself as Seth.

Most extraordinary about this incident is that Seth apparently emerged as a separate personality.[21] He began describing himself and the spirit world and answering many question about man, God, and the universe. Realizing the possibly incredible implications of these sessions the Robertses decided to continue them. Soon Mrs. Roberts had only to put herself into a trance and Seth would take over, Mr. Roberts writing everything down. Reading this material afterwards, Mrs. Roberts was always amazed. Not only did she admittedly lack such knowledge, scope, and vocabulary, but occasionally had difficulty understanding many of the concepts. Following Seth's instructions, the Robertses compiled the information into a book called *The Seth Material,* then into another *Seth Speaks,*[22] and others, Seth even recommending a particular publishing company which indeed published her early material.[23]

---

[21]Jane Roberts, *How To Develop Your ESP Power* (New York: Frederick Fell, 1966), pp. 18-19.

[22]Jane Roberts, *Seth Speaks* (New York: Bantam Books, 1974).

[23]Roberts, *How To Develop Your ESP Power, p. 8.*

SPIRITUAL EXISTENCE

What strengthens the possibility of Seth being a separate personality from the spirit world rather than a product of the Robertses' imagination is that on one particular occasion Seth purposely materialized his spirit in the physical world, like a ghost. Two of Mrs. Roberts's students also saw the same manifestation or apparition,[24] and Mr. Roberts, an amateur painter, ultimately painted Seth's face. That the Robertses mentally created his image accidentally is possible, although such indiscriminate projections are rare and purposeless. Again, accepting Seth for what he claims to be, a spirit from the spirit world, is simpler, more logical, and complements other similar findings about such matters.

The purpose of this book is not to sensationalize extraordinary incidents such as this, Mr. Monroe's excursions into other dimensions, or the incredible testimonial evidence Dr. Moody's patients offer but rather to show how information from different sources corroborates the life after death hypothesis and offers important clues to the spirit world's nature and other dimensions beyond physical life.

For example, both Seth and Robert Monroe claim that thoughts govern much of the spirit world, a difficult but extremely important concept to imagine. In other words, whatever we think becomes real, spiritual reality looming just as functional and significant as physical reality, perhaps even more so since spirits are not restrained by the body or subjected to physical deterioration or physical death.

During separation, if Monroe thought about sunning himself on an ocean beach, for example, the scene would exist and he would be there. Likewise, when Seth decided he needed a rural setting where he could work he purposely created, mentally, a fourteenth century study. Taking a physical form, he retreated

---
[24]Roberts, *The Seth Material, pp. 115-121.*
[25]Roberts, *Seth Speaks,* p. 48.

61

there to sit at a desk and look out the window. Of course, "work" must be interpreted here as mental work, possibly some form of meditation.[25]

Though difficult to imagine in these particular cases, beach and cottage do indeed exist, though not physically as we understand and perceive in our world, but in Monroe's and Seth's minds respectively. Arguing that physical reality is the only true, real one because we exist here or because our five senses tell us so looms more and more like narrowmindedness, if not simply arrogance. This attitude is comparable to Seth or another spirit arguing that *their* world is more real or the only dimension simply because *they* exist or perceive there.

Interestingly then, hypocrisy, lying, and other such deceptions are impossible since thoughts cannot be concealed, and the hateful, the evil, the immoral, the malicious, the violent, and those exhibiting stress or tension will undoubtedly carry such attitudes into the next world, possibly maintain them forever, creating their own eternal hell. Since mental pain is considered worse than physical, the implications of all this cannot be underestimated.

Conversely, the truly moral and loving, particularly those from group three, will unquestionably fair quite well, except for initial adjustment problems. Speaking through Ruth Montgomery (author of *A World Beyond*) in much the same way Seth does through Jane Roberts, the spirit, Arthur Ford, implies that our evilness or goodness are apparently felt in the next world just as is true here.

Robert Monroe also substantiates the fate of those carrying even slightly negative thoughts into the spirit world after physical death. He had difficulty adjusting in the spirit world when he first began separating. Even his most guarded fears, inhibitions, and desires manifested themselves almost uncontrollably.

SPIRITUAL EXISTENCE

My first visits to Locale II brought out all the repressed emotional patterns I even remotely considered I had—plus many I didn't know existed. They so dominated my actions that I returned completely abashed and embarrassed at their enormity and my inability to control them. Fear was the dominant theme—fear of the unknown, of strange beings (nonphysical), of "death," of God, of rule-breaking, of discovery, and of pain, to name only a few.[26]

Jane Roberts also agrees. Her depression during one particular separation manifested in the spirit world as a horrible dog-like creature chasing and attempting to bite her. Only by willing herself back into the body did she manage to avoid the terrifying experience, and even consciously felt the effects afterwards.[27]

This is very important information if the spirit or soul lives forever, which seems so, since our existence in the spirit world will depend on the precise nature of our consciousness. Concerning such immorality, the soul, unlike the physical body, is not subject to age or deterioration, one reason why time seems continuous in the spirit world, ever in the present, or simply nonexistent. That the spirit or soul is indestructible is perhaps comparable to the concept that energy cannot be created or destroyed, just altered, like producing carbon monoxide, dioxide, and other chemicals from burning gasoline. Similarly, the spirit is probably one of many byproducts the body releases after physical death.

The reader might wonder how we could have problems in the spirit world if it is so peaceful, quiet, and loving, possibly containing such loving spirits as the being of light, and so on. To answer, the spirit world's general characteristics are one matter and how souls respond to or are compatible with its probable

---

[26]Monroe, p. 77.
[27]Roberts, *The Seth Material,* pp. 177-179.

numerous dimensions of existence, much less other spirits, is another, again depending on the nature and characteristic of the soul's consciousness, what area of existence it enters, and other factors.

But while the immoral, the unethical, and the stress-filled people generally function on earth without fearing the consequences, the situation seems quite different in the spirit world. Although loved ones will reportedly greet us there after physical death, family ties appear less significant, and whether or not a soul will remain at the same level of existence with another family member will depend on the nature of his consciousness — an extremely important characteristic of spiritual existence and being — and other factors.

Several religions and philosophies suggest the idea of spiritual levels, including Buddhism. The theory is that after physical death we will exist in or at a particular plain, perhaps considered as a level of development, depending on the nature of our characters and/or goodness. The more moral and loving we are, the higher the level; the less moral, the lower, and many levels supposedly exist.

Describing dimensions of existence beyond physical life is difficult because language is geared for *this* world, and knowledge about other realities is scant. But *levels* seems inappropriate and inexact because the word conveys *layers,* which is misleading. Testimonial evidence doesn't suggest layers or earthly concepts of *high* and *low,* presupposing positions on a kind of scale. Considering modern investigation, *areas, sections, frequencies, planes, dimensions,* or *worlds of existence* seem more precise and will be used interchangeably throughout this book.

Monroe has supposedly penetrated or perceived various areas of existence. Many of Dr. Moody's near-death patients and others had glimpses of such areas. Because of arrogance, egotism, ignorance, or brainwashing, and because the physical world seems so real, many have difficulty accepting the possibility that our world is only one of many existences, much less possibly a lower form.

In addition, referring to existence after physical death as "the next world" rather than "worlds" also seems inaccurate because many areas of spiritual life are thought to exist. These areas are probably unique, unlike the confining, limited home of the physical body which, in turn, is the spirit's confining domain. In fact, concerning the latter, many revived near-death patients report having experienced feelings of great freedom and mobility following separation.

Though we could conceivably exist forever in the spirit world, there is no guarantee that we will never reincarnate into another physical body on earth later, or even in another body on another planet in the universe, once again depending on many variables, particularly including the nature or level of consciousness we reach after physical death or even later in the spirit world.

Reincarnation into lower forms of existence (a cow or insect, for example) seems imcomprehensible since our consciouses are too complicated — powerful, if you like — to enter and reside in a lower creature's brain. Any such attempted entry would undoubtedly "blow the set." In addition, such reincarnation would require styling down the consciousness — removing acquired knowledge and awareness — to fit the appropriate creature. Having lived as a human being, what could we possibly learn incarnating into a cow? (That such incarnation could be punishment for past evilness once again implies that a creator is unjust enough to punish us for imperfection He is indirectly responsible for, since He created us.) Such incarnation sounds negative and purposeless, contradicting our development and particularly our general purposes on earth.

Though he wasn't referring to reincarnation, Oliver Wendell Holmes's statement that "a mind stretched by a new idea can never go back to its original dimension" seems applicable. Man undoubtedly evolved from a simple cell, his oldest ancestor, and has been logically developing and progressing toward what he is potentially capable of becoming (whatever that might be), not regressing, as reincarnating into lower forms suggests.

Testimonial evidence suggests that, observing our lives pass before us at physical death, we judge ourselves. This seems far more logical and just, and it would appear that the creator would have to be at least as just and fair as any good, moral man, if not more so. It also seems fair that we then have the opportunity to make proper adjustments and improve ourselves in spiritual dimensions or reincarnate into some physical form later.

Seth maintains that despite our beliefs, all of us have probably reincarnated and probably will again.[28] Arthur Ford also agrees, along with many, many others. Since the extraordinary Bridie Murphy case during the 1950s, there have been so many cases of regression to supposed former lives through hypnosis that the experience is almost common knowledge, although not everyone can be hypnotized.

Those arguing against reincarnation cry "cryptomnesia," implying that under hypnosis such people merely recall bits of information that they have seen, heard, or read somewhere but have consciously forgotten. The information is then recollected during regression. But how such people are able to speak different languages (xenoglossy) or play the piano during such regression without consciously knowing either remains a mystery. Better yet, it can easily be explained by reincarnation.

Why or how some individuals do or don't use other tongues to describe former lives during regression is the biggest mystery but again might depend on individual differences. For example, Betty and Mary are Americans. Regressed back to former lives,

---

[28]Roberts, *Seth Speaks,* p. 5 and Roberts, *How To Develop Your ESP Power,* p. 18.

Betty, professing to be a German during the twelfth century, described that life in English. Mary, professing to be Swedish during the fifteenth century, described it in Swedish.

Accepting the idea of reincarnation, some psychiatrists treat patients for problems supposedly carried over to the present from former lives revealed through hypnosis. Their occasional successes don't necessarily prove reincarnation indisputably of course, but strengthen other information already supporting it. Westerners tend not to accept reincarnation because the theory contradicts most of our religions.

Returning to our original discussion, it seems logical that the next world contains various areas of existences and actually approximates physical life more than we realize. Spiritual life seems different only because perception, travel, communication, and other functions differ from those in physical life.

We are generally unaware of areas of existence on earth but they *do* exist, although in different terms, barely noticeable because the body camouflages our consciouses or spirits. For example, generally speaking we tend to associate with certain people because our consciouses are compatible. We dislike being with those possessing dissimilar feelings and attitudes, though sometimes we are forced or in some way feel obligated to associate with them for various reasons. Therefore, areas exist wherever or whenever we converge with others. Likewise in the spirit world, except that we lack bodies and probbly will not feel so obligated, much less to converge or communicate with anyone unless we so desire.

Consider hypothetical Bob, a typical human being. He relates to a certain group of people and perhaps feels closest to one or two whom he calls his good friends. He refuses to accept Jack into his consciousness (the same as saying that Jack isn't his friend) because Jack tends to lie, is vicious, deceitful, hypocritical, and so on, contradicting much of what Bob is. But because Jack might be a relative, co-worker, or employer, Bob, like many of us, feels compelled to associate with him though he dislikes even being near him.

This situation creates tensions and problems for Bob and others like him who have attempted to adjust in a complicated, difficult world. In one sense, Bob would have been better off being born centuries later when and if the world did not contain men like Jack, although, in another sense, this world and its problems are perfect for the kind of learning and developing Bob needs, although he is unaware of this.

Continuing this hypothetical case, let's assume that Bob was quite idealistic when young. Rejecting the materialism and false money values of his times, he actually considered quitting college and running off to live alone in the woods. This would have been a worse choice because potentially good men like Bob (candidates for group three) should be involved with society to help improve it and to grow intellectually, emotionally, and spiritually themselves. It is probably through such men that the superintelligence and consciousness can work.

Living in the woods wouldn't have taught Bob very much, although at the time he wasn't aware that it wouldn't. Having "overadjusted" to civilization (sometimes called "conformed"), he is presently less aware of what he calls his "rebellious past," and suffers from the usual stresses and anxieties of everyday living.

Bob has many possible courses of action concerning Jack. He could tell him off and suffer the consequences, possibly even get fired if Jack is his employer, or cause a major rift in his family if Jack is a relative. Because Bob is generally fairly reserved, easygoing and friendly, and dislikes causing more tensions, bitterness and ill-feeling that he already endures, he remains quiet for a time.

But one day his consciousness reaches a point where he decides on a new approach. Appealing to Jack's morality or consciousness, he reproaches him for a hypocritical, deceitful action toward one Mike, and uses every means to change Jack's general behavior (consciousness), but to no avail. In fact, Jack ultimately tells Bob to mind his own business, and repeated efforts to change Jack end similarly.

The situation will undoubtedly be entirely different in the spirit world. Assuming that both consciouses remain unchanged at physical death, Bob probably will not want to remain in Jack's company for long in the spirit world. Were Jack a relative, Bob might greet him there, or vice versa, depending on who died first. But not even family ties could bind these incompatible consciouses. Just as on earth, Bob will ultimately seek and attract spirits compatible with his consciousness, so will Jack in the spirit world.

Certainly Bob might offer his love or even try to help Jack as he did on earth. Jack might even call for help, and spirits might indeed offer it, since love apparently holds everything together. But if Jack rejects that love or help from Bob or others, or plays his hypocritical, deceitful game, the good spirits will have no other choice but to discontinue such help, or simply ignore this worthless spirit until or unless it changes. This could take centuries of earthly time, or never occur at all, in which case Jack could conceivably forever exist alone or in an area compatible with his nature, one which would negatively complement and embellish his consciousness. Depending on his consciousness, he could even exist in an area comparable to hell.

The incredible point is that unlike on earth where immoral individuals *can* and *do* survive and function, perhaps even quite well, this isn't true in the spiritual worlds. Because Jack's consciousness is based on lies, hypocrisy, and deceit rather than truth, justice, love, and other worthwhile qualities, his contribution to the spirit world would probably be nil. In fact, he would become a deterrent to general spiritual development, and spirits would surely have to avoid him simply out of self-preservation until and if he could work out his problems and begin improving morally.

Chapter V

Religions and the Creator

Man's consciousness has developed to the point where most of us are truly aware of the Bible's many inconsistencies and half-truths. Therefore, we are hypocrites for accepting it as God's word. Unless we are willing to agree that God's consciousness isn't much better than Jack's, for example, many of us can only wonder how a supposedly great God can be so petty, jealous, and unjust as the Old Testament depicts. Furthermore, if Bible critics are devil-inspired, then so are all intelligent, informed, unbiased men seeking similar truth about God.

Religions are generally quite inaccurate, inconsistent, contradictory, and even immoral. For example, how can we preach "Thou shalt not kill" on the one hand, then support war and killing on the other, as men have throughout history? Worse, how can supposedly informed, intelligent people believe in and follow so-called religious leaders who say one thing, yet do another? How can such leaders talk about giving to the poor and following Jesus' simple, humble ways when they have amassed gigantic fortunes and live worldly, materialistic lives?

How or why we tolerate leaders who preach the virtue of giving to the poor and underprivileged or simply helping them while their own religions greedily hoard or cling to enormous wealth is an incredible mystery. Do we really think that God or Christ could possibly condone such a contradiction which truly amounts to immorality? As humans we're remarkable for possessing great intelligence and innovation on the one hand but an amazing knack for trying to fool ourselves on the other.

Some religious leaders are no more guilty of acting out such incredible contradictions than many of us who blindly believe in and follow them. Such men become leaders and flourish only because a particular type of mass consciousness supports and reveres them. Initially their intentions were probably good and generally still are. Matters simply got out of hand. Seeing no way out (and perhaps enjoying their material comforts and power), they have merely accepted their situation like many of us caught up in everyday trends, conditions, or general mental attitudes. Unfortunately, they are victims of their own decadent, materialistic times.

Admittedly, their preachings *do* offer some hope for those who are oblivious to their religious leader's flaws or contradictions, even when others point them out. But sometimes their followers will resort to violence defending such inconsistencies, waging war against the so-called disbelievers, the enemy, or the evil ones, as they have throughout history. Unfortunately, the scant spiritual help such leaders and religions stimulate can never compensate for the ignorance and fear they perpetuate and sustain.

True, religious leaders like the Pope are particularly responsible and beneficial for bringing many people closer together harmoniously, spiritually, and lovingly. But unfortunately, many such people are secretly convinced that *only* such leaders are infallible or capable of direct communication with the creator. We all have the potential of tuning in and communicating at least with those in the spirit world, if not the creator, if we could only eliminate our stresses, disassociate from antiquated religions, change our attitudes and values, and become spiritually good—no easy task, I realize.

Testing if your religion is truly moral, good, tolerant and loving, assuming you follow one, ask yourself to consider as seriously and objectively as possible if it ever made you intolerant, unloving, suspicious, hypocritical, or deceitful toward those of another faith, as following a particular religion often does, intentionally or not. Has your religion or its ministers caused you grief, unhappiness, or stress? Has it prevented you or anyone from marrying someone of another faith, race, or color, for example? Does the creator really have a preference? Has following your particular religion caused you to fear God, frightened you about hell, or made you feel guilty about so-called sins that you cannot seem to control because of any number of reasons? Despite what your religion has supposedly taught you, do you still fear death? Has your religion made you feel impure, evil, inferior, or convinced you that you might ultimately suffer eternal agony in a horrible domain called hell? Have you been led to believe that you're not a so-called chosen one?

Has your religion convinced you that the money, time, or whatever that you give toward its organization is really for God or that God will reward such sacrifices? Is your religion advocating or in any way stimulating, directly or not, dislike or hatred for the Catholics or Protestants in Ireland, for example, the Moslems or what Westerners might consider strange religions like Buddhism or Hinduism? What about fostering dislike for nations or groups?

Does your religion control any aspect of your life, advising you what foods to abstain from or eat or when? Do you follow what you secretly consider are absurd rituals and practices, hoping to gain favor with the creator? Because of your religion, do you feel obligated to recite or chant at specific times words that you hardly believe, understand, or even stop to consider?

Such rhetorical questions are almost endless. If you have answered any of these affirmatively, you should seriously consider rejecting your religion altogether. If it isn't partly or completely immoral, spreading evil, pessimism and ignorance or brainwashing you, it's stunting your spiritual growth and hardly preparing you for the next world.

One evening I watched a fairly accurate television version of the Old Testament story concerning Sodom and Gomorrah. Most of us recall how, according to the Bible, God's angels warned Lot and his family to flee Sodom which God planned to destroy along with Gomorrah for supposedly being corrupt, worldly, and sinful. (Here, again, simple people are left with the incredible responsibility of clearly discerning that these are God's messengers, not the devil's.) The angels also warned Lot's family not to look back at the city as they left. But Lot's wife did, and was turned into a pillar of salt for disobeying God's direct command, which some Bible scholars and religions consider the worst sin. (In fact, some also claim that for disobeying God's command not to eat the forbidden fruit, Adam and Eve are either residing in hell or aren't eligible for earthly resurrection.)

To say that either fate is unjust and unloving is sublime understatement. The punishments are simply too severe for the crimes. After all, Lot's wife, Adam, and Eve are simply imperfect humans. Such punishments are comparable to a parent killing a child for disobeying a rule. Once again, perhaps the greatest injustice of all is to blame or portray God as behaving unfairly when, in fact, the story is unquestionably man's. By destroying Sodom (an example of extreme violence) along with all its in habitants, God Himself contradicts His own sixth commandment, Thou shalt not kill. To repeat, evilness, violence, and hatred only breed the same, and any implication that the creator possesses such base faults is too illogical and incomprehensible for intelligent consideration.

The creator's consciousness unquestionably operates on a higher, more complex level of morality. Whether a single or multiple entity, it is logically and unquestionbly all-knowing, all-just and all merciful. We cannot be morally greater than it or we would all be gods. I'm not saying that we cannot aspire to achieve greater levels of morality and consciousness. In fact, our underlying purpose in life should be to strive for perfection in every area, from sweeping the floor to building a city, and particularly concerning spiritual and moral matters. *We should strive to be greater than we are in order to achieve the fullest potential of what we are capable of becoming.* That many of us hardly consider striving for perfection, however, unless we receive some form of remuneration, praise, power, or glory in undeniable. The Bible is meaningful to whomever accepts it, unquestioningly, for whatever their reasons. Conversely, it is obsolete for those whose consciouses recognize the flaws.

Chapter VI

Thought-sustained Dimensions of Existence

Many spirit worlds exist beyond our physical world and are probably sustained by thought. In fact, one probably exists as a kind of duplicate of our world but in spirit form, according to Seth, Monroe, Arthur Ford, and others, Monroe reportedly visiting such a world during separation. It contains streets, homes, cities, and people—souls or spirits.

Explaining its existence is simple but perhaps difficult to accept initially. Spirits from those physically dead appear to will such dimensions of existence out of strong desire or need for them. In other words, because many people undoubtedly had difficulty accepting physical death, they merely attempt to function as on earth. Consequently, their combined thought power picturing, desiring, or willing the physical world into being, creates and sustains it in the spirit world. Thought power probably maintains the brilliant city of light which George Ritchie describes in *The Vestibule,* for example.

Discussing a possible duplicate dimension of existence or a world like ours always stimulates tremendous curiosity and many questions. Students in class usually wanted to know if America exists there, along with the energy crisis, cars, sports, alcohol, and so on. They also ask if spirits feel pain, have sex, and so on.

The answer is a guarded yes to most of these and many related questions, but requiring careful explanation because of certain differences. To illustrate, consider Bill, another hypothetical case, who has an unexpected heart attack and dies in his early thirties. Separation occurs, and from a distance Bill observes various people working on his physical body, confusing him, because he has no conception of what happens after a physical death, except what he learned in his youth during Sunday school and from others, amounting to little or distorted information. In fact, he doesn't even realize he's physically dead. He perceives the dark tunnel, watches his entire life unfold before him, and sees the being of light.

Though all this is quite unusual, Bill simply shrugs everything off, which he usually did about similar important matters during physical life. In fact, he quickly reverts back to his normal, carefree, unspiritual self. Invariably finding solace and comfort in various bars on earth, he thinks about a bar, and the thinking creates it. He expects to see the usual: the bar, the bartender, people drinking and talking, and he does, since all this is in his mind. He orders a beer, and the bartender complies. He reaches for the glass, unaware that he's seeing with "astral eyes."

Because such activity was so natural for him during physical life, he simply lifts the glass to his lips, drinks, and his mind handles the rest. He swallows, tastes, even feels the cool liquid traveling down his imaginary esophagus. He feels refreshed or how he would normally expect to feel during physical life after drinking a glass of beer.

Since Bill isn't overly imaginative, the bar will be typical of the kind he normally frequented during physical life. It will be plush, dingy, or whatever, depending what his concept of such places was during physical life. The possible images and/or events that have occurred and will follow are infinite, depending on his level of consciousness, and his normal thinking, which also affects how long he will remain in this plane or, in this case, "attitude" of existence.

Picturing another beer, it suddenly appears like magic or as in a dream, before Bill even considers calling the bartender, the first noticeable difference between physical life and the spirit world. Though somewhat surprised, he immediately assumes someone bought it for him. Curiously, he glances at the various people at the bar, but really couldn't care less who was responsible and quickly pictures a beautiful woman drinking alone. What was wishful thinking during physical life now becomes a reality.

Startled by her ravishing beauty and sexy figure, Bill wonders why he hadn't noticed her before. Assuming she must have just arrived, he begins eyeing her. Because he wants her to accept his advances and actually anticipates that she will, she does. In fact, imagining himself sitting beside her, he is immediately there. Calmly, he accepts the physical unreality of all this (particularly because it is pleasurable so far), just as we do in dreams, and continues, hardly considering how incredibly clear and physically real everything seems. So engrossed in her beautiful face, he hardly considers the episode a dream, since no part of his awareness signals that it might be.

He speaks quietly to her. She responds exactly as he thinks she should in this mentally contrived experience. Eventually he pictures having intercourse with her at her apartment and is immediately there doing so. Still undaunted because of his character, (how he would have normally responded to a similar situation during physical life) he merely finishes, and the incident seems harmless at first.

But carefully examining the incident turns up many possible problems and ramifications. For example, relationships based only on physical attraction are rarely satifying or at least as meaningful as those based on love. Since Bill only wanted to satisfy his biological needs, he will receive a comparable return on what he was capable of expending of himself, which isn't much and mostly negative, based on his level of consciousness. Although he didn't ask if she were married, he is suddenly curious because this thought is connected to another lurking in his subconscious, and he imagines she is. In fact, he must now deal with the other thought, that of an angry husband arriving home and finding them in bed. Because this very scene was a frequent daydream during physical life, with Bill actually working out the different possibilities and consequences, he happens to recall one in which a husband removes a gun from the drawer and aims it at him. This now becomes a spiritual reality.

Only by pleading for his life and imagining that the man is merciful, does Bill manage to escape with his life, spiritually speaking. Had the husband shot and wounded him, Bill would have suffered whatever pain he normally would have expected to feel in such a situation, depending on where and how badly he thought he was wounded.

Had he imagined himself dying, Bill would have experienced whatever was his conception of death, including pain, hell, or possibly total nothingness, if he believed death was final. In fact, if he believed in the latter, much effort by him and/or other spirits would probably be required to awaken himself from what would probably be defined as a self-imposed, nonfunctioning kind of dormant consciousness.

The situation could stimulate other negative possibilities. Instead of the husband routine, Bill might suddenly realize how easy it was picking up this woman. Speculating that she has venereal disease, he suddenly would have it, and in any particular stage that he might suddenly imagine out of fear, or recall from what he read in books, watched as a serviceman, or heard about.

Of course, the incident could have ended positively or happily, one might argue, but only if Bill were secure and well-adjusted, which is inconsistent with the type I have purposely portrayed. Certainly a different human being possessing a different consciousness would avoid this entire incident and its consequences.

Whatever negative religious training Bill might have acquired from his youth could now torment him. Raised to believe that fornication is sinful, for example, he could will himself to hell by the slightest fear of being sent there for punishment. Hell would then become whatever his conception is of that domain, including the usual pictures of horror, stench, and eternal suffering, and he would suffer whatever discomfort and pain he thinks he should under the circumstances.

Certainly he could have conceivably willed himself away to peaceful surroundings but only if he learned that he can do this in the spirit world. Of course, fornication and other so-called sins shouldn't be condoned, overlooked, or not labeled for what they are simply to avoid what effects such acts might have on the soul in the next world.

I deliberately chose to illustrate a series of simply, hypothetical images and events that could have happened to any consciousness like Bill's following physical death. Because these images and events weren't true during physical life doesn't prevent them from happening when Bill arrives in the spirit world or make them any less real. He could have also experienced all this during a near-death experience, then choose whether or not to explain it after being revived. He could also forget it, consider it a bad dream, be too frightened to mention it, and so on, explaining why near-death information is scarce but important.

Apparently spirits sharing similar thoughts and possessing the same level of consciousness can form patterns of reality or types of spiritual existence. In fact, we can and often do create unusual trends, attitudes, feelings, and so-called phenomena right here on earth if and when conditions are right because we create our own environment and worlds, as Seth repeatedly mentions.[29]

Concerning Bill again, the combined power of many spirits imagining a bar, the beautiful woman, and various customers could have structured and maintained all this in the spirit world where other spirits could venture if desired. Bar and surroundings could last forever, depending on the powers creating, believing in, and sustaining them.

They could will such a bar into existence because their attitudes (their levels of consciousness) haven't changed much since physical life when they enjoyed such places. In fact, like Bill, they might be unaware that they're physically dead, although such ignorance isn't absolutely necessary. They might simply enjoy such drinking and socializing, as unfruitful and unproductive as it would be there and frequently is here, depending on types of spirits involved. Those noticing differences or desiring different existences or functions would probably leave, penetrating more appropriate planes compatible with their attitudes and development.

Other areas probably exist, operating and functioning according to the combined energy, attitudes, and thought power from spirits in their group. Such areas could contain anything and everything, from spiritual manifestations of the Wild West to dimensions of chivalry and knighthood and so forth. Accidentally penetrating the latter without realizing physical death has occurred, a modern day man's spirit might conclude that something was definitely wrong, unless he thinks he is dreaming.

Eventually and hopefully, he will accept and understand such dimensions for what they are and avoid or penetrate them,

---

[29]Roberts, *Seth Speaks,* p. 20 and Roberts, *The Seth Material,* pp. 109 and 123.

depending on the nature of his consciousness, what he wishes to do in the spirit world, and other variables.

Aside from the obvious, the major differences between the physical and spiritual worlds is that in the spirit world we generally appear to pool spiritual energy, working together harmoniously to accomplish certain tasks, including creating and holding various dimensions together. In contrast, we generally go our separate, unloving ways during physical life, forever competing and struggling to fulfill materialistic and egotistical ambitions.

Chapter VII

Dimensions of Hell

The combined thought power of many spirits believing hell exists could have created and still be maintaining it. Spirits convinced they should be in hell as "punishment" for certain "sins" such as missing mass, profaning God's name, stealing, lying, and worse crimes like rape and murder are probably holding it together, although this alone is probably not the only amalgamating force.

Disbelievers in hell are better off, even if they aren't sorry for wrongs committed during physical life, lessening their chances of willing themselves there. The point is that all of us make mistakes because we're imperfect creatures and are still developing. Surely we can't or shouldn't expect to go to hell for them.

Where we might reside — what plane of existence — is hard to say and mostly depends on the nature of our consciouses — how we think, feel, and what we believe at the moment of physical death. Most souls still have much to learn or unlearn, especially if they possess anxiety and stress, are unloving, or feel no remorse for physical wrongdoings. They will possibly require much counseling in the spirit world, meditation, and/or more physical reincarnations to overcome such imperfections.

Reading Ruth Montgomery's book, *A World Beyond*, I was surprised at first when Arthur Ford implied that Hitler apparently isn't residing in a plane comparable to our conception of hell. If anyone deserved hell because of the tremendous suffering he caused, Hitler does.

Already resigned to reconsider the idea of souls willing themselves to dimensions like hell, I decided to check Hitler's life. Baptized a Catholic, Hitler rejected Catholicism and all other religions, having no qualms about sending priests and other religious leaders to concentration camps.[30] Hitler was an atheist, neither believing in heaven nor hell, which explains why he probably couldn't or wouldn't have willed himself there.

But he is not off the hook so easily, nor are we, if we don't feel remorse for our physical wrongs. Like all of us after physical death, he lives with his own thoughts and images, except that his fate is a thousandfold worse than ours because of the enormity of his evildoing. Once again speaking through Ruth Montgomery, Arthur Ford describes Hitler's fate in the following excerpt which I quote completely because of its importance:

> Let us take the case of a Hitler, who seems to have wrought so much evil in one lifetime that he will never again be able to cleanse himself of such evil. He comes here after wrecking the lives and hopes and ideals of many other souls in the physical state, and he himself is an object of such scorn and horror that no one mourns his passing from the physical state. Here he thinks to resume his antics, his goosestep, his prattlings of power, but there is no one to listen or pay homage. This soul is so totally ignored that it is as if he were alone in a dark island without habitation. He prances, rants,

---

[30]Prof. Willilam A. Jenks, "Adolf Hitler," *The World Book Encyclopedia*, ix, p. 236.

shouts, to no avail. There is none here so low as to seek association with this monstrous soul. Shouting and strutting achieve nothing, so at last he falls into a deep pit of his own image-making, and into the black pit he falls, falls, falls until, like [Edgar] Cayce tells of Saturn, he is in outer darkness. There he is left to his own devices for many hundreds, perhaps thousands of years, depending on the severity of his crime against humanity. If he ever wakens again, his fate will not be a pleasant one, for until he has repaid at least some of his crimes against others by long and arduous study in this state of being, he will not be offered an opportunity again to return to earth life where progress would be faster. He has doomed himself to isolation for many eons, and the fate of Hitler will not be known to any of you living today, for his banishment—self-banishment, if you will—will undoubtedly take much longer than anyone now living in the flesh can perceive.[31]

The question now arises as to where Hitler's henchmen are residing, such as Goering, Goebbels, Himmler and the rest. Why aren't they with Hitler since they believed so fervently in him during physical life?

I didn't check their lives, but if they weren't atheists, they might be existing in hell if they believed in it. If not, once again determining their exact whereabouts in the spirit world would be as difficult as pinpointing where anyone is on earth at any given moment. Logically, they might have called and willed one another together (although not necessarily, just as we don't necessarily continue to fraternize with one another on earth because we are friends, co-workers, or relatives), then separated, finding little comfort in one another, or were simply too confused to organize at all.

Possibly less evil than Hitler, they might not have wanted to be with him. But they too could be existing separately, possibly

---

[31]Montgomery, pp. 81-82.

worse than suffering in hell with souls of comparable evil, or they might be locked in the deep sleep of nothingness which Arthur Ford calls the sleep of shock.

Though speculating about infamous people is probably interesting, what is more important is understanding that hell can not only exist in one's consciousness but definitely as a separate dimension. *Beyond Death's Door* by Dr. Maurice Rawlings is extremely significant. Not only does it offer similar testimonial evidence supporting Dr. Moody's cases but also explains why none of his near-death patients reported experiencing or perceiving anything even closely resembling what we consider hell.

According to Dr. Rawlings, most near-death people naturally tend to remember their pleasant experiences rather than unpleasant ones. Nor are they very anxious to reveal incidents suggesting that they might have gone to hell and are therefore destined for such a place. Consequently, he suggests interviewing near-death patients immediately after they are revived, lest they forget the incidents. Doing that, Dr. Rawlings has reported receiving just as many similar negative experiences as good ones from near-death patients, or just as many glimpses into so-called hell as heaven.[32] Such excursions might not only be warning the particular near-death patient to live a more moral, loving physical life after he is revived, but signaling all of us.

Dr. Rawlings also discusses Dr. Ritchie's book, *Return from Tomorrow*. Dr. Ritchie described a journey with a spirit being he identified as Christ. The being showed him a number of "worlds," one of which, that of the damned, lay on what appeared to be the surface of the earth. Here "depraved spirits were at constant warfare with one another. Locked in personal combat, they punched and gouged at one another."[33]

---

[32]Maurice Rawlings, M.D., *Beyond Death's Door* (Nashville: Thomas Nelson, Inc., 1978), pp. 20-22.

[33]George G. Ritchie, M.D., *Return From Tomorrow* (Waco, Texas: Chosen Books, 1978), pp. 63-64.

Because of the "planes" or worlds" that Ritchie saw exist in other dimensions, they could be anywhere, including superimposed upon the physical world and even before us although we can't perceive them under normal conditions. They also could be close to earth or even inside it, as Reverened Kenneth E. Hagin implies in his supposed journey into hell during a near-death experience.

Reverend Hagin had a heart attack on April 21, 1933 and immediately found himself descending. The deeper he proceeded, the darker and hotter it became until he observed flickering lights on the walls of what he described to be "the caverns of the damned." A giant orb of flame seemed to draw him toward that place, despite his efforts to resist.

Reaching the bottom of a pit, he became conscious of "some kind of spirit-being" at his side which, interestingly, he doesn't equate with Christ although, being a priest, one might have expected him to. Then again, he was so engrossed or frightened by what he called "the fires of hell" that he never looked at him. The spirit-being laid a hand on his arm and escorted him in. Eventually, he describes how a power pulled him away from the fire and heat and into the shadows of darkness. He soon began to ascend until he reached the lights of earth and described how he slipped right back into his body the way he went out, through the mouth.[34]

Notice how the reverend describes the separation, reentering his body through the mouth, the way he left. As mentioned earlier, no two separations or even near-death experiences seem exactly alike, because of individual differences, and apparently the consciousness or soul can reenter (and seemingly leave) the body anywhere, or, at least according to how each person wishes or seems to perceive it.

---

[34]Rawlings, pp. 108-109.

The account is particularly interesting because he describes himself descending into a hot region, approximating the popular version of hell and its location. But because perception is slightly different during separation, to consider this description in physical terms, i.e., that hell truly exists somewhere "down there" in the earth, would probably be a mistake; "down there" is probably the best way to describe passing into another dimension. True, the center of the earth is undoubtedly molten hot. But that hell should truly be there rather than any other place, would be too coincidental and difficult to justify or even imagine.

The next logical consideration is determining if this hell was simply in the Reverend's mind, like Seth's study or the bar in Bill's case, or a separate dimension in the spirit world. The "spirit being" seemingly offers the key. That the Reverend could have accidentally imagined what appears to be the very type of "spirit being" described by many of Dr. Moody's near-death patients and countless others years later, seems too coincidental. "Spirit beings" and such dimensions of hell seem to exist outside the Reverend's mind.

Again, this spirit seems to be just that, a spirit wishing to show the reverend a glimpse of one particular dimension comparable to hell.

In his book *Oregon's Amazing Miracle,* author Thomas Welch also describes a place that appears to be hell, which he experienced during separation after a near-death experience. This account also appears in Dr. Rawlings's book. What Welch saw was a "burning, turbulent, rolling mass of blue fire. . . . A lake of fire and brimstone. There was nobody in it. I was not in it."[35]

Although Thomas Welch recognized people who had died earlier, none of them actually seemed to be in the fire. They

---

[35]Thomas Welch, *Oregon's Amazing Miracle* (Dallas: Christ for the Nations, Inc. 1976), p. 8.

were all looking at it as he was, confused and bewildered by it. Then Thomas Welch saw a man "coming by in front of us. I knew immediately who He was. He had a strong, kind, compassionate face, composed and unafraid, Master of all He saw. It was Jesus Himself."[36] Jesus simply looked at Thomas Welch and in "seconds I was back entering into my body again."[37]

This experience also seems to exist separately, outside of the mind because it is similar to other accounts where a near-death person encounters a spirit being's presence. Precisely why people are looking at the "blue fire" is difficult to determine, but we can speculate. Perhaps they were raised to believe in hell and feel they belong there because of guilt, anxieties, sins or fears carried over from physical life. Or perhaps they were truly revengeful, unrepentent, hateful souls who accepted hell as their fate after seeing their lives pass before them following physical death.

But because they're not punching and gouging one another in personal combat as in Ritchie's account, their plights have possibly followed another, quite familiar pattern. First, they might not have realized or understood they physically died, causing the original confusion. Unaware of the separation and other phenomena following physical death, possibly they tried to function in the spirit world as they did on earth, discovering certain inconsistencies, causing more problems and confusion.

Even had they accepted physical death, perhaps they were having difficulty operating in the spirit world because of little or wrong information. They might therefore have accidentally willed themselves to this particular plane, not realizing how or why, compounding their predicament, otherwise why would they be there, unless one still wishes to maintain that God judged and sent them there for punishment? Possibly they re-

---
[36]Ibid.
[37]Ibid.

main because they don't know how to will themselves to other, more desirable planes.

Whatever, their situation is extremely sad and unfortunate since their physical deeds probably did not warrant such a predicament. The spirit accompanying Dr. Ritchie, for example, reacted predictably to equally lost souls existing at a similar plane, showing "nothing but compassion and unhappiness that these people sealed their own doom."[38]

Dr. Rawlings's book contains similar glimpses of what appear to be different versions of hell; therefore, which is the real hell? Or, more precisely, which plane is the hell that physical man has discussed and feared throughout the ages?

The answer has to be all of these hells. Apparently enough souls have been and still are willing to hold such planes together or they wouldn't or couldn't exist. Again, that these particular planes of hell are worthless or contradict universal harmony or the creative or love force is sublime understatement.

Blaming the superior consciousness for purposely creating these horrible planes of hell seems unfair and illogical since they serve no constructive purpose. Even the average person, were he God, possesses more compassion and morality than to have purposely created such negative domains, and God's sense of justice and morality is undoubtedly greater. The only other logical force responsible is ours — our varied thought power, our thinking patterns stemming from collective spirits believing in and thinking in terms of hell. Particularly applicable here is Seth's often repeated idea that we create our own environment and worlds, here and in the next world.[39]

Apparently too many souls from the physical world have been and still are arriving in the spirit world, "confused,"

---

[38]Ritchie, p. 64.

[39]Roberts, *Seth Speaks,* pp. 45, 65 & 69 and Roberts, *The Seth Material,* pp. 112-124.

"bewildered," or simply evil, and their consciouses are actually sustaining hell and other worthless planes. Should the number of such souls in the spirit world continue to increase, they could ultimately overcome the loving spirits.

Such souls, in turn, could return to physical man through reincarnation, further corrupting him via the inner self, and the cycle would continue. Moral degeneration on earth would spread like cancer and become the rule rather than the exception. Crime and violence would increase, eventually becoming uncontrollable, especially since the police would naturally become just as evil, violent, and corrupt. Finally, the world of Hitler would be child's play in comparison.

Since loving thoughts apparently hold all forces in the universe together, including the spirit world,[40] everything would be affected: everything would become chaotic and collapse. And who knows if this actually didn't happen in still another dimension at a different moment in time. And who knows but that somehow one strong, loving consciousness managed to escape such chaos and ultimately become our superconsciousness, our God, bringing with Him all that He had learned from a previous existence, including some knowledge of evil or simply some imperfection which He has been struggling to purge through man and other regenerative life in the universe?

Much of what I have been saying does, in fact, parallel the Bible. I never said the Bible was wrong but, rather that it reflected man's consciousness at the time it was written, and since the prophets lacked our sophistication and knowledge, they certainly could not have gone into the kind of detail concerning physical life and the spirit world offered in this book. Nor could they discuss prophesy, or interpret "divine inspiration," messages from the spirit world—God if you like—in any other

---

[40]Arthur Ford days that love "is the glue that binds us all." See Montgomery, p. 29.

way than they did, which the morality of the times influenced.

In ancient times people had enough difficulty understanding and following Jesus' teachings or any similar spiritual giant, much less understanding anything from a concept such as "the separation," to the "thought concept" which we have difficulty understanding or accepting today.

It now seems clear why near-death people have visited negative planes of existence as well as peaceful, loving ones. The spirit world's message to physical man is not simply: "You'd better be good or you might go to hell," but involves much, much more. What they appear to be saying is: "Begin to prepare for the spirit world by first understanding its nature, then understanding the serious consequences of living a stress-filled, unloving physical life. These consequences might not only be detrimental to your own everlasting spiritual life, but contribute to the destruction of our peaceful, loving planes of existence, along with the harmonious, loving system of things, including the superconsciousness. And time might be running out."

Why didn't the different spiritual guides simply spell all this out to near-death visitors instead of showing them different glimpses of hell? Such warnings seem negative, dictatorial, fear-instilling, unloving, and smack of direct interference, very different from letting souls from all different walks of physical life draw their own conclusions and letting man develop at his own speed. Such spiritual objectivity is also consistent with Dr. Moody's being of light who hardly communicates with near-death people when their lives unfold before them, much less warns, scolds, or even judges. In fact, I have never read about any spiritual guides (the being of light and others) who were anything more than noncommital and were simply there as aids, or perhaps what many of us have called "guardian angels."

Chapter VIII

The Religions and General Consciousness of Group 2

Today, particularly in materialistic societies, many of us lead superficial, wild, licentious, unspiritual lives, comparable to the Israelites until Moses supposedly gave them the Ten Commandments. Following careers and pursuing jobs, we have become slaves to the dollar and what it buys.

Many of us have lied for money or material gain, or eventually will. Many even swindle, cheat, sell their souls for such gain, and we're never satisfied. Our greed and selfishness are insatiable and grow unendingly, frequently causing financial difficulties and bitterness within families and a multitude of other problems which cause much unhappiness.

Caught in this rat race and hoping to get more out of life, many turn to alcohol and drugs, attempting to alter consciousness and chemically escape. The mugger, the thief and other supposed misfits and undesirables are always wrong, we argue, yet the capitalistic value system stresses the importance of money and what it buys, causing the less endowed or less fortunate to do anything to acquire the same.

More police and more severe punishment for disobedience aren't the solution to the problem of increased crime. If we could somehow de-emphasize our materialistic values and become truly loving, good, and spiritual, then, stealing, mugging, and other crimes would probably become unthinkable. Such antisocial acts would be inconsistent with the general attitude or level of consciousness. In fact, if our society were truly loving, we would satisfy the material and spiritual needs of the destitute, the jobless, the misguided and confused, not just discuss their plight, offer token help, or manipulate them for political gain.

The selfish, the unloving, and those materially better off forever offer excuses for not helping the needy. Money and jobs are always available for them so why should they worry? All we need to do to increase the supply of money and jobs for all is change our priorities and have some imagination. In other words, we need only become less selfish and more loving.

Religions only compound our problems. Their teachings are frequently based on ancient traditions and laws, hardly applicable to our changing times. In fact, only when church attendance begins declining do various religions suddenly become hypocritically innovative, changing their formats and even their philosophies to increase attendance. Religions offer absurd answers, little hope out of the rat race, and plenty of contradictions and hypocrisy. Many people subconsciously realize this but simply accept their religion anyway because they feel so helpless and lost.

In fact, many people attend church out of habit, guilt, fear of death, or because they think God will reward them — give them a better seat in heaven because they were good enough to take time out from hectic lives to attend church. Some secretly believe they will be rewarded for mumbling endless, hardly meaningful words (prayers). Many have never even taken time out in their lives simply to understand what their prayers mean, much less feel or believe them.

Many people are aroused, excited, and inspired by various sermons, particularly the fire-and-brimstone kind that promise that God will one day judge us or that we're all destined for hell. True, coupled with beautiful, inspirational choir singing, such sermons can inspire believers and those desperately wanting to believe in Jesus, God, and the afterlife. But they can also work people into such religious frenzy that they become emotionally fixated about exaggeration and half-truths forever, carrying such beliefs and attitudes into the spirit world, a very seirous and irresponsible situation.

Surrounded by such an atmosphere in massive, expensive, highly ornate churches containing the usual idols, people have even passed out in joyous ecstasy. At some religious services, people have also been known to speak unusual language (called "the tongues") which others claim they can immediately interpret, convincing still others that this must therefore be the true and right religion or that only they can communicate with God and vice versa.

That the creator and/or Jesus caused this ecstasy or stimulated this language and that this must therefore be the right church and faith are highly improbable assumptions; yet, many are convinced about both. If any one religion is correct, God has certainly made it difficult for man to determine which it is from the many that exist, nor has He led us into choosing the right one.

He hasn't because there isn't any right one; man has simply devised his own religions to satisfy his needs (or fears). The various conditions: the sermon, the emotionally piqued around us, the music, the church's awe-inspiring architecture are more likely responsible for arousing us, not God or Jesus.

Attending any particular church or following a particular faith isn't a prerequisite for becoming emotionally or spiritually inspired, although many secretly believe that such attitudes or feelings (state of consciousness) cannot be reached independently. The point is that the more such people listen to such sermons and allow themselves to be brainwashed, the more difficulty they will have in breaking away from antiquated concepts. Such brainwashing, emotionally inspiring at the time, leaves us with the usual negative fears about God, judgment, and hell which can seriously affect our transition into the spirit world after physical death.

Christmas stimulates excessive paganism, hypocrisy, wholesale greed, competition for material goods, gluttony, increased drinking, and probably more sexual promiscuity than normal, and we're forever condoning, excusing, or attributing our behavior to Christ's birthday (all the more reason why we should behave more morally than usual). If supposed happiness, holiness, and good cheer, et cetera, are our aims, why not pursue them throughout the year, as Jesus would have wanted? Observing our behavior at his supposed birthday, which probably isn't December 25th, Christ would probably be appalled. Besides, though many people get emotional during Christmas, singing carols and attending mass (once a year for some), few really think about Christ or what he really accomplished, much less emulate him by becoming more loving and spiritual.

Lying, cursing, cheating, and so on are bad enough, but fooling ourselves into believing that attending church or mouthing some prayers will erase such faults is hypocrisy sublime, a fault which few religions consider sinful. If hypocrisy isn't simply lying, it's deceiving others, oneself, and is phoniness. We won't be able to fool anyone or play hypocritical games in the spirit world where others will readily perceive our thoughts. Also, if we haven't overcome hypocrisy by then, we'll have difficulty communicating ideas accurately, since hypocrisy disguises truth and stunts growth, no matter where we are.

Arriving in the spirit world we will be what we are, in other words, at what level of consciousness we have reached upon physical death, nothing more, nothing less, and we won't suddenly become all-good, all-just, sincere, or whatever if we haven't been so on earth. Once physically dead, all we can hope to experience is remorse about what we failed to become during physical life (since remorse at least implies recognizing faults) or pride if we were, or struggle to be, morally decent.

We frequently rationalize our anger, nervousness, insincerity, revengefulness, jealousy, lying, and other faults. We frequently blame them on our hectic jobs, those around us, our complex lives, our parents, children, friends, our youth, society, and so on, but rarely ourselves. Nor do we see ourselves as others see us, as we really are, mostly because of our incredible egos. Careful self-analysis will clearly show that there is no real basis for possessing such faults. They can truly be overcome if we are willing to make certain adjustments, change our perspectives, our values, and be more loving. Considered differently, somehow we should be able to overcome our own inadequacies, faults, and problems, although sometimes with the help of others.

Life is so complex, that discussing the many problems people face daily is difficult. But there's something very wrong if we are constantly shouting at or are upset with our children, friends, relatives, employees, collegues, whomever, or if we are constantly lying, hating, or acting insincerely.

Everyone's life is truly his own, not God's, both here and in the next world even though the creator indirectly gave us life. But there is no evidence suggesting that the ultimate power directly interferes in our lives. Therefore we should judge and analyze ourselves and make any needed changes now, not after watching our lives pass before us at physical death when it's too late.

Feeling remorseful about our failings will not only be redundant but a dangerous attitude to carry into the spirit world. It could force us to reside at an undesirable area of existence. In addition, we might not necessarily be able to overcome such imperfections in another life, since we are rarely conscious of faults from a previous life. If fact, we might not have the opportunity to reincarnate for centuries, or at all, if man destroys himself in the meantime.

Chapter IX

Meditation

Our general emotional reaction toward material things is sometimes incredible. Not only do we hoard and attach great importance to such, but overreact when we or someone else accidentally breaks something we own, even though such behavior won't repair or replace that object or cure our carelessness or that of the person responsible. In fact, our behavior toward others (sometimes even toward ourselves) creates more stress, fear, unkindness, and sometimes even hatred.

Living highly complex and frequently hectic lives is probably responsible for our frequent edginess and impatience with ourselves and others. In our efforts to pursue our careers to earn money, we sometimes have little time or energy to discuss matters calmly with others. This again reflects a lack of love, with stress a contributing factor. Our impatience grows proportionally to the complexity of our lives; therefore, we are frequently quick, unjust, hard, and unkind because we live complex lives.

meditation can be as simple as closing the eyes and thinking. Transcendental Meditation seems quite logical and very appealing, requiring us to think or review our thoughts during meditation, a seemingly natural and logical step since thinking is automatic. With our eyes closed, the mind begins to consider future, present or past events, images, problems, ideas, hopes, fears, probabilities, and so forth. Considering such matters offers us the opportunity to fully contemplate what we probably should have done more thoroughly before but didn't because of any number of possible reasons (including lack of time or too many distractions), causing hidden stress. Closing the eyes while meditating prevents distraction by surrounding objects, even people, if we're forced to meditate near others or amid noise.

Thinking about things tends to undo the stress surrounding them, although, strangely enough, we don't necessarily decide or assume beforehand what events or problems have been causing stress, then purposely think about them during meditation. The mind, an incredible organ, will naturally single out what takes priority, some thoughts undoubtedly emerging from deep within the subconscious or inner self.

Sometimes during meditation one dwells on some seemingly obscure or supposedly meaningless thought — an incident, an unkind remark, a personal problem — that occurred years ago and was supposedly forgotten. Having most likely been causing stress without the person realizing it, it now surfaces, demanding attention. In fact, considering such a thought becomes quite pleasurable because the thought is receiving the kind of attention it should have received before. Thinking about it undoes it, alleviating some stress. And so it is with other thoughts; meditation alleviates more and more stress until one's attitude about himself, others, and the world begins to change in new, exciting, and wonderful ways.

At the time this book was written, I had been meditating for about five years. Most of my thoughts are now concerned with

Teen-agers admit to me that they lie to their parents, which they justify, claiming parents are too strict, old-fashioned, indifferent, too preoccupied with other matters, unfair, and so on. Many teen-agers get away with such behavior and attitudes not because parents are stupid, but mostly because, so overburdened with stress, parents simply cannot handle serious involvement.

Dealing with stress itself becomes a complex and highly charged situation. Several alternatives are possible. One is to find a stress-free job. Unfortunately, this is probably impossible, if not unrealistic for many. Another alternative is to seek psychiatric help, since discussing problems alleviates tension and stress. But this is simply unaffordable in most cases.

A carefully worked-out exercise program can help reduce tension. So can jogging or walking but both are time-consuming.

Meditating is by far the most practical solution to stress. Unlike exercise programs which frequently require equipment, using a gym, or enduring bad weather, it can be done almost anywhere. Meditation *does* alleviate stress. In fact, consistent daily meditating will probably completely eliminate stress.

Serious meditators constitute a small percentage of the world population, probably less than one percent in the United States and the entire Western world.[41] Some people hardly understand meditation, much less its many different types. Others are convinced that all meditating is difficult, un-Western, or some kind of alien religion. Still others equate all meditation with Yoga, various types of breathing and unusual body posture, and they reject it completely.

Though some types of meditation demand total obliteration of all thoughts until a blank mind is achieved, no easy task,

---

[41]Harold H. Bloomfield, M.D., *Transcedental Meditation* (New York: Dell Publishing Co., 1975), p. 36.

the present or future because I have long since reviewed most past stressful matters, including long-forgotten incidents from childhood.

The philosophy behind TM (also referred to as the science of creative intelligence) or any meditation is that freed from stress, one will function better, be more creative, feel happier, be more tolerant of others and be in harmony with the natural world, God, and others.

During meditation, transcendental meditators silently utter a two-syllable word called a mantra. Though one can meditate without saying the mantra, monotonously repeating it quiets and lulls the body into relaxing without deliberately ordering it to do so. Pulse rate and other vital signs examined before and after meditating substantiate that the body does, indeed, quiet down and rest during meditation.

But saying the mantra shouldn't take precidence over considering one's thoughts, since simply uttering a word doesn't relieve stress. Such utterings should intersperse one's thoughts, and one shouldn't worry how often to say the mantra or when. Sometimes I become so engrossed with my thoughts during meditating that I forget to say it. On several occasions I recall afterwards not having said it at all.

TM teachers claim that only they have the necessary qualifications to assign students proper mantras, supposedly based on personality and other factors. Most refuse to explain how the words are assigned, as though it were some forbidden secret. In fact, students are asked to promise never to reveal their mantras, even to fellow students. Undoubtedly awed or perhaps even frightened by totally unnecessary and certainly exaggerated mysticism surrounding TM, most students comply faithfully.

The monotony of silently reciting any meaningless, two syllable word seems to quiet and relax the body. The reader can manufacture his own or choose any of the following: say-la, herem, may-vim, day-na, ray-lin, shal-lay, ray-far, and so on. However, meditation can be accomplished without using a mantra, although, perhaps, not quite as effectively. What is vitally important though is *disciplining* oneself to meditate at least twice daily and not expecting quick results. One should meditate before eating, preferably before breakfast and dinner, since digestion tends to accelerate the heart, defeating the quieting and lulling effect.

People who rise early for work are the hardest to convince that awakening even twenty minutes or so earlier to meditate will ultimately make them feel better, fresher, and require less sleep. The thought of rising even earlier can be disconcerting to many, but I guarantee that if one meditates correctly and faithfully, stress will be alleviated, indirectly providing more energy so that a person will require less sleep.

Following is a list of some of the benefits, not necessarily in the order of importance, one can expect to derive once he has begun alleviating stress through meditation:

1. He will feel less nervous and edgy.
2. He will be able to tolerate emotional and physical pain better.
3. Meditating slows down the body functions, enabling one to rest the heart (during meditation), unquestionably adding years to physical life.
4. Alleviating stress enables one to have more energy, be more vigorous.
5. Food will actually taste better, go down easier.
6. One becomes more tolerant of others — *more loving.*
7. One will begin to have a new, better perspective of life and the world, have fewer periods of depression, for shorter durations, and be less negative. In fact, meditation tends to curtail and possibly even *eliminates* depression.
8. Meditating gives one the opportunity to get into the world of himself; *one learns to know and understand himself better.*
9. Alleviating stress will improve concentration, memory, possibly even intelligence.

10. Most importantly, by alleviating stress, the consciousness will be less apt to be in a state of confusion at physical death and thus have a better chance of landing in an area comparable to one's calm mental state, rather than one comparable to hell.

People can successfully meditate anywhere, even amid noise as long as it isn't jarring or disconcerting. People have been known to meditate in subways, airplanes and trains. I prefer meditating sitting alone in a quiet room, although sounds such as traffic noise, doors slamming, or barking dogs shouldn't interfere.

Beginners sometimes inadvertently concentrate on outside noises, but with practice and patience, they will eventually be able to focus on their thoughts. Others ask if they can listen to soft music while meditating, which is possible, but I see no sense in purposely introducing a possible distraction.

One shouldn't answer the telephone or door unless absolutely necessary and unavoidable, and certainly not open his eyes or begin talking to anyone during meditation. Once resumed, such interrupted meditations always seem less effective, even if one meditates longer. To meditate properly, one should sit erect in a chair without slouching or supporting the head with a pillow, hand, or anything else.

Meditation provides needed rest and energy and can replace mid-day naps and retiring early, which can be inconvenient or sometimes impossible. Sometimes I fall asleep during meditation (from anywhere from five to twenty minutes, although some doze longer, which is perfectly normal) because I didn't get enough sleep the night before or worked too hard during the day. Determining how much longer to meditate after such dozing depends on individual differences and other variables, such as time and need. I usually prolong the session by about ten minutes. Some people fight against dozing during meditation, which isn't necessary; others never fall asleep, indicating they're rarely tired, which is possible, depending on their lifestyles. Here are the precise steps to follow when meditating:

1. Sit comfortably and quietly in a chair. Wear a watch or face a clock so that you can periodically check the time by peeking through one eye, rather than completely opening the eyes. (It is only necessary to check the time when you begin saying the mantra during step #3, not during the shorter periods which can be approximated.)
2. Close your eyes. Think about anything you like or allow any thoughts to enter your mind. (1 minute)
3. Begin interspersing your thoughts by saying the mantra if you decide to use one. If you don't use one, continue to examine your thoughts. (15 minutes)
4. Without opening your eyes, stop saying the mantra if you're using one. Stretch if necessary. (2 minutes)
5. *Slowly* open your eyes. Simply sit quietly, getting your bearings. (1 minute)

Meditation is finished. The process is simple, but the problem is disciplining oneself to do it consistently, for the rest of one's life. This sounds demanding but it is worth the little time required, considering the far-reaching benefits. We think nothing of sleeping for many hours. Meditation is comparable to sleeping, but far less time-consuming and actually helps reduce sleeping time.

Meditation isn't a panacea for all ills, of course. We certainly can't expect to function perfectly just because we meditate if we abuse the body by hardly sleeping, taking drugs, eating poorly, or drinking excessive alcohol. Yet meditation can help those who pursue these habits. They eventually will begin to feel better and less tired.

Precisely how soon one can expect to notice benefits from meditation is difficult to determine because of many variables such as the extent of one's stress, daily exposure to stress, one's physical and mental condition, how a person treats his body, and so on. Although I found meditation immediately relaxing, refreshing, and enjoyable, I didn't begin observing personal changes until after about two weeks, and they were very subtle and minute. Real improvement occurs slowly and in small doses but it does occur.

To illustrate, after two weeks of rising earlier to meditate, I had more energy than before and needed less sleep at night. I also began falling asleep quicker, easier (not mulling over thoughts handled during meditation) and sounder. Situations seemed less disconcerting, threatening, irritating, or tiresome at home or work.

After months of meditation, my concentration seemed keener and I was able to retain more information. I was also developing far more tolerance for others, despite their faults. Having reached a certain level of calmness, I suddenly realized how truly nervous I had been. Others began noticing changes in me, particularly my family.

Stress-free, we become more tolerant and patient, and I was becoming a better listener as months of meditation continued. Cumulative upset, worry, and tension apparently created what had always felt like a knot in the pit of my stomach, a possible forerunner of ulcers. This also disappeared. The uptight feeling I invariably experienced after driving long distances also vanished.

I had always considered myself fairly secure. Meditating helped me feel even more so. In fact, I now believe that what I frequently evaluated as personally threatening or sarcastic behavior in others might have only seemed so, viewed by my stress-filled mind.

Today I seem able to analyze others' behavior clearly, for precisely what it is. Most unkindness, for example, springs more from anxiety and stress than from inherent evilness. Realizing this, I'm more able to cope with such abuse, although no one appreciates being treated unkindly, of course. I try to have more understanding, sympathy, and love for stressful people than for those with less stress or none since they suffer from their own tension plus that which they attract from others.

At the risk of sounding immodest, I can now perform any physical or mental labor without becoming upset when problems arise, and only become mildly bothered, perhaps *disappointed* is a better word, when I, or anyone else, accidentally scratch, break, or temporarily misplace a material object.

I have always striven for perfection in all areas and still do, but mental errors cease to disturb me as much as before. Meditating for many years has helped me become more tolerant of physical pain and helped me to evaluate man, the world, and God better, from a new, deeper, more realistic and enriching perspective. I awaken each day happy to be alive in the physical world, happy to tackle the day's activities with optimism and enthusiasm.

Some argue that continuous meditation can be so calming that a person becomes impervious to everything and everyone. Meditation unquestionably changes one's character. A person invariably becomes far more tolerant of people and life's difficulties than before, but how can this be considered anything but an important plus, possibly even a matter of remaining physically and mentally healthy, if not alive, and extending physical life? This benefit *has* to be superior to developing an ulcer or heart trouble from stress.

Meditating certainly hasn't made me indifferent to everything and everyone. In fact, I consider myself the opposite or I wouldn't have written this book. Meditating has helped me handle potentially stress-filled situations to such as extent that I hardly avoid them, as I might have before.

Critics of meditation also maintain that the aggressive, the domineering, the unkind and the angry can humiliate and take advantage of the usually low-key meditator. I question this contention. Meditators are usually so tuned in and in harmony with God and the spirit world that they have long since attributed such behavior in others to stress or an underdeveloped conscious. Rather than storm back at stressful people, which can only compound their negativism, the meditator can invariably function normally without getting upset and with far better results than before. Meditators undoubtedly affect others very positively. Facing the calm personality of the meditator, others invariably back off, become less obtrusive, even more loving.

As humans, it isn't necessarily our responsibility to "turn the other cheek" toward the mean, the unkind, the unjust, and the stress-filled, since such people probably wouldn't (couldn't) respond to such behavior, but only take advantage of it. Perhaps our responsibility is to criticize them for their faults and possibly call them what they are, whether liars, cheats, mean or hypocritical, rather than get upset keeping such matters to ourselves which can be *extremely* difficult, especially if we are emotionally involved with such people. But if we don't make others more aware of what they are or how they behave, how can we expect them to change and improve?

Others argue that we all can't be like Jesus Christ. Yet all of us possess his attributes as a man, including his potential for moral perfection, and therefore should strive for it. If all of us would really make a concerted effort to embody Christ's teachings, instead of fanatically idolizing him, the world would undoubtedly be better.

I believe it is crucial for us to be conscious of what we are so that we can strive for positive improvement in every area and become more of what we are potentially able to become so that we can function better in the physical world and be prepared for the spirit world. Meditation can help us achieve these goals.

Chapter X

Visits from the Spirit World

The ouija board is not magic. It is merely a board containing letters and numbers and serves as a medium through which certain spirits can communicate with us. Time of day, night, or season and whether or not a room is dark or light apparently have little bearing on the ouija board, save that darkness tends to frighten participants more. *Where* such sessions are held could be important, depending on the nature of whomever lived in a particular house before. The participants' consciouses — their frames of mind — also seem to be an important variable. Poor results are achieved if the participants are nonbelievers or closed-minded, the opposite if they are not, the latter unquestionably "permitting" certain connections or manifestations to be made through or in conjunction with them. Apparently such spirits are either unaware that they are physically dead or are so attached to earthly matters that they welcome the opportunity for such communication. Breaking or destroying the ouija board can be so disconcerting to them that they somehow manage to manifest a sound of crying or screaming in the physical world, seemingly emanating from the board, or so many people have reported to me.

I realize such claims are as difficult to accept as their explanations. But I have heard so many similar reports about sounds supposedly coming from tables owned by deceased relatives or rising ouija boards or tables that it's difficult to write them off as figments of the imagination. Unfortunately such sounds, along with manipulation of objects and peculiar manifestations of ghosts or incidents of psychokinesis have been so exaggerated in popular novels that many intelligent people close their minds to *any* possible penetration into the physical world. Such gross exaggeration forestalls serious consideration of legitimate, unexplained phenomena.

The following incident occurred when I was eighteen. It exemplifies not only the manifestation of sound in our world (by some unknown force which I can only consider negative or nonconstructive at the very least, if not evil, because it frightened us) but also the consequences of using the ouija board or any similar medium unwisely or at all. Those unfamiliar with the idiosyncrasies of such mediums shouldn't use them, and since few people seem to agree how such devices actually work, particularly the ouija board, I guess that means all of us.

One late summer night, two friends and I were walking home from a high school dance. My house was empty because my parents and sister weren't home. My friends and I decided to work the ouija board in my room. We had experimented with the board several times before but this time we planned to request that some sign or communication be given to us, indicating the devil's presence or existence.

We placed the tips of our fingers lightly on the base of a cocktail glass placed upside down on the board, the pointer having been lost. We started by asking simple yes and no questions concerning high school romances, sports, and the weather. It wasn't long before the glass began answering quickly, sliding back and forth quite well. I remember that every time we bluntly asked for a sign from the devil, the glass immediately stopped, and dead silence prevailed.

One of the others and I were very curious about this experiment. The third continued fooling around, secretly thumping the floor or wall in an effort to simulate a sign. Only after we repeatedly admonished him did he finally stop. We resumed the insignificant questions in order to activate the glass, interspersing them with the burning question. Nothing happened for at least a half-hour. Several times when we asked for a sign we thought the window shade extended outward from one of the two open windows, but we attributed this to the wind.

"Show us a sign from the devil," we asked still again, and suddenly it happened. An enormous sound, closely resembling that of heavy chains, erupted. Something began dragging, starting at one corner of the ceiling as though someone or something was pulling chains along the attic floor above, and continued at the same pitch toward the other side.

Three panicked teenagers never evacuated a room faster, crawling, falling, bumping into one another at the door, racing down the hall, fumbling, finally grabbing the upstairs banister, then descending two and three steps at a time. Half-laughing and shouting hysterically, we finally arrived in the kitchen, frantically opened the back door, and flew outside. We ran for blocks before stopping to collect ourselves. We tried to understand what really happened but couldn't except simply to attribute the noise to the devil.

Still trembling, I finally walked back to the house after trying but failing to persuade the others to walk me home. I sat on the curb outside my house, glancing furtively at my lighted bedroom, straining for a sound but hearing nothing as I waited for my parents and sister. When they arrived, they were surprised to find me outside, but I gave them some excuse for being there and followed them inside. I wasn't about to venture upstairs until they did! When they finally went up to the second floor and nothing happened, I followed suit. Everything in the room was as we had left it. Shakily I put the ouija board away, resolving not to use it ever again (and never did until many years later). Nothing further happened in that room that night or ever, though I can recall occasionally awakening from a deep sleep, soaked in perspiration, anticipating something frightening about to happen.

My parents responded predictably when I told them about the incident the next day, laughing and blaming it on our overactive imaginations. Not until many months later did I muster up enough courage to examine the attic and only then with my cousin during broad daylight, when everyone was home.

There is no way that such a tremendous noise could have been made by natural causes, such as a limb falling from a tree, or a rat, squirrel, or any other animal running across the floor or on the roof. Except for a few cartons of stored books, the attic room above mine was essentially bare and also lacked anything metallic. Furthermore, nothing had been disturbed or knocked over. In fact, pursuing the idea that a "natural mishap" caused such a tremendous noise is absurd. The premise that we simultaneously imagined it is equally impossible. The chance of three people doing so at any particular moment must be astronomical.

The point is that we later unanimously agreed that the sound had truly resembled dragging chains and nothing else, a significance difficult to explain except to say it was negative (born of negative intentions) for having frightened us, and that chains have frequently been associated with enslavement throughout man's history. That we ourselves were mentally responsible for producing the sound is difficult for me to accept, since none of us specifically thought about chains.

Interestingly, this chain dragging did, in fact, succeed in accomplishing what we consciously or subconsciously wanted — to be stimulated or thrilled, the same reasons many of us watch certain television programs or movies. The lesson this provides is that if we can request or tune into something negative and under certain conditions "receive" a like response, why not request the positive, as I did in my daughter's case? The key phrase is "under certain conditions" which, unfortunately, seem to vary from one situation and one set of participants to another.

Had we truly communicated with the so-called devil and had he created this sound? Again the "devil" label presupposes many complicated possibilities that are difficult to answer completely. Perhaps there isn't a spirit called the devil, per se, but simply one particular spirit existing in some area of the spirit world who embodies all the negative characteristics that man imagines, dreams, or in some way comprehends. He could also be the evil spirits' leader, the anticreator. Rephrasing the question, could there be a spirit who, having somehow continually reembellished his own evilness through repeated physical reincarnations, is now the epitome of evil? The answer would have to be very likely, and he could very well be the leader of all the other evil spirits we have simply named "the devil."

Surely there is no way of knowing positively that the sound was inspired by the "devil." In fact it probably wasn't, since there is no more reason for the evil spirits' leader to respond to such an insignificant request than there is for the creator to respond to important, positive requests such as prayers for peace or pleas to save lives. The devil's concerns probably involve far more negative and evil matters, and one or more lesser evil spirits probably created our sound. Or, considered still differently, whatever force (call it "evil," "the devil," "spirits," or whatever) wanted to create or was capable of creating such a sound did indeed create it in the physical world or somehow in our minds, ruling out that physical chains were actually manifested and then dissolved, a considerably more difficult feat to accomplish. Such stories are so common that I'm surprised that we are so slow in drawing important conclusions from them. This is partly, I realize, because we lack the proper scientific equipment to analyze and understand such pehnomena. Scientists invariably require consistent and repetitive results under controlled conditions, which isn't always possible. One major stumbling block is that a force might choose to manifest chain dragging on one occasion, rattle the shade the next (and it could be a different force or spirit), or do nothing for the next fifty sessions or even centuries. If spirits are responsible, which is more than likely, the point is that their behavior is as unpredictable and infinite as ours in the physical body.

The owner of a rug business, an acquaintance of mine, was working alone on a job, one night, nailing down a carpet in a vestible. Hammering away unsuspectingly, he was suddenly surprised when someone or something began hammering back, underneath, initating his strokes in about the same area, every time he finished a nail, and just as loudly.

Curious, he rose, entered the living room where the lady of the house was sitting, and asked if anyone else was in the house, particularly downstairs. Puzzled, she answered negatively. He explained what had been happening, and both soon descended into the basement to investigate, walking directly underneath where he had been working. Like the attic in my experience, the area was bare except for a stud leaning against the wall (which, I suppose, could have been responsible for creating the noise, had some force chosen to utilize it or was capable of doing so).

Both returned upstairs. Already feeling ridiculous, he tried to duplicate the incident in the lady's presence but to no avail. Whatever or whomever had been responsible, ceased, altogether. Feeling even more ridiculous, he finished the remaining work and left soon after. Why the strange hammering wasn't resumed, is difficult to determine and once again is based on the unpredictability of such behavior. Nothing like that ever happened before or since, in all his years of laying carpets, he said.

Apparently some spirit, force, or forces once again were able to make some connection or penetration into our world, possibly using him as some kind of agent or catalyst. How it could have done so seems hard to explain, again, but perhaps we can speculate why I must attribute this sound to something intelligent such as a spirit, rather than some manifestation of energy.

Whether spirits are summoned by the ouija board, through mediums, or choose to manifest themselves in other ways, there seems to be a number of reasons why they are trying to communicate with us. I will list the main ones below because they might help explain many other similar cases. It is also important to realize what I have been alluding to all along—that we are like spirits in the spirit world except we're still housed in the physical body in the material world. In other words, *we* are spirits, except we're not in the spirit world yet, having chosen to reincarnate in physical form. But despite where we exist, we are what we are because of the level of consciousness we have achieved through various physical reincarnations or whatever. I will use *it* in referring to spirits since the male and female concept is probably non-existent in the spirit world.

1. The spirit wishes to tell us something about the spirit world.
2. It's probably unaware of many characteristics about life and death, including the fact that physical death has occurred. Confused and trapped on earth, it's struggling to get our attention, hoping we can help it function properly or help it understand its dilemma, unaware of how limited we are in

helping them here. Its situation is rather hopeless and unfortunate because most of us would hardly recognize such a contact or penetration, would be too frightened if we did, or would blame it on natural causes or imagination. Nor would we possess the knowledge, desire, or love to try to help it.

3. It is a negative or "evil" spirit, such as the perpetrator or perpetrators of the dragging chains, wishing to frighten us.
4. Because of its nature or level of consciousness, it enjoys teasing, comparable to the practical joker in the physical world. It might or might not be truly trapped on earth. Whatever, its pranks serve little purpose.

Although cases of good spirits trying to communicate with us abound, the antics of the bad, trapped spirit or evil forces are frequently more memorable because of their frightening, negative impact. This is why I continually emphasize that only constructive, purposeful, and positive ouija board and séance experiments should ever be attempted.

Trying to contact souls of the dead to learn if they still love, hate, miss us, or are sorry they mistreated us while on earth hardly seems meaningful. Some people have been known to struggle for years, at great expense, in an effort to contact spirits of spouses or business partners, asking permission to remarry or opinions about major decisions respectively. Others, trying to get tips on winning horses, stocks, and business ventures, seem to have a false sense of values and should consider reevaluating their consciouses. Such matters are hardly spiritual concerns, and we shouldn't try forcing or involving spirits in them, especially because they might be struggling to develop more worthwhile attitudes and concerns. They will send us their love energy if they desire or if and when such is within the scope of their consciouses. But the closer a spirit remains to earthly matters, the more it risks the chance of becoming trapped and remaining here forever.

Learning to accept a loved one's physical death is truly difficult, but something we all must face during physical life. Fortunately, we can anticipate meeting loved ones in the spirit world, possibly even working and existing together, providing our consciouses are compatible. On the other hand, once in the spirit world, we might not want to remain together, lacking anything in common with a former "loved one" whose soul is now completely revealed to us and contains serious flaws. Or it might reject us for the same reason. In addition, that loved one might have long since chosen to reincarnate, and for the time being doesn't even exist in the spirit world.

The good or well-adjusted spirit operates differently and generally wouldn't use a ouija board or séance as a vehicle for communication unless for constructive, positive ends. Great spirits like the beings of light or Christ would probably never involve themselves with mediums.

Unless preoccupied with truly more important matters beyond our comprehension, good spirits unquestionably think about and send us love energy, just as we will most likely do once arriving there. Some people, for many reasons, hardly know when they receive such energy, especially if they possess considerable stress. Others might attribute any exuberance or energy felt, to themselves, others, situations, coincidences. moods, nothing, or hardly even consider such matters.

Unexplained footsteps, slamming doors, mysterious whisperings in the cemetery, and apparitions are probably due to trapped spirits (ghosts). Even if they are pranksters, such spirits are usually in trouble because they shouldn't be in the physical world.

Such penetration or attempted penetration is comparable to us trying to enter the spirit world, which obviously contradicts physical existence. People like Robert Monroe and others who purposely enter the spirit world after *willed* separations usually understand the consequences of their actions and know that they are truly physical beings temporarily journeying in the spirit world. Ghosts and confused or trapped spirits (usually one and the same) invariably do not understand their predicament, an extremely important and critical difference. It isn't that ghosts or trapped spirits particularly enjoy inhabiting (haunting) castles or older houses but that a greater number of people having inhabited older homes over the years increases the likelihood that some spirit might not have made the proper transition after physical death and still exists there for its own reasons.

One particular story I heard is quite significant because the information gathered supports many of this book's basic premises. A student whom I will call Martha told me that her family had been experiencing some very unusual occurrences since her Uncle Randy had been killed in Vietnam when Martha was about five years old. The entire family was convinced that Randy's ghost had been haunting their house since then, meaning that they thought his spirit was probably trapped on earth.

A spirit chooses to inhabit one house instead of another for very good or at least justifiable reasons, mostly because of its relationship to any or all of the members of that house or what might have happened or didn't happen there. Certainly there are exceptions because such spirits are restrained, and we're discussing the unpredictability of behavior. Important in this case is that Randy and Martha had been very close when Randy was alive; or, more precisely, Randy apparently loved Martha very much and also had a good relationship with Martha's younger sister, Claire, and the rest of the family.

The usual odd incidents had been occurring in this house: unprovoked door-slamming and footsteps, the family members insisting that they could "feel a presence" which they concluded was Randy. The climax of many unusual happenings at the house centered around a recent snapshot showing several family members standing near a sofa in the living room during the Christmas vacation. The photo was clear except for a strange, shadowy substance, like smoke, visible near Randy's service picture hanging on the wall above the sofa. Had Martha not continually (and privately) reported to me the strange events that had been occurring at her house, I probably would have attributed the shadow to faulty film, developing, or the camera, and simply dropped the matter.

Teaching such a course, I couldn't afford not to capitalize on this opportunity and decided to assume that the shadow was, indeed, Randy's supposed attempt to materialize in the physical world. The point is that some spirits are better at such materializations than others (which I attribute to individual differences and other factors), just as some of us are capable of penetrating the spirit world while others cannot. Some spirits are even capable of materializing clear faces and bodies of themselves and have even been known to speak.

Since students had been urging me to try the ouija board in class and the course was nearing completion, I finally consented because of an ulterior motive involving Martha and Randy, which I didn't reveal to her or the class. Martha consented to be one of four participants along with several other good, intelligent, reliable students. Once we got the pointer moving, I would try contacting Randy's spirit, I announced.

Everything seemed right for the experiment. The class and the participants were curious, serious, and believed that the ouija board worked. Additional factors were apparently in our favor, which I didn't discover until later. For example, Randy not only had attended this very school, but had taken English in this very classroom, though not from me.

Up until these ouija board sessions, I had always been skeptical, like most people, about the ouija board (despite the chain-dragging incident), séances, and related mediums. Since the students were reluctant to ask the questions (perhaps embarrassed, unsure, even frightened), I volunteered. If contact was made, assuming that Randy was a reasonably decent spirit (not particularly negative, evil, or a prankster), possibly he could answer what I considered important questions at the time.

In other words, if his answers didn't support my concepts either: (1) I was wrong, (2) Randy was wrong or was simply unreliable for any of many possible reasons, or (3) the participants were deliberately moving the pointer. From my line of questioning, I was convinced that I would be able to tell which of the three or any combination was true. Because of what ultimately happened, I'm convinced that none were and that a contact had, indeed, been made with Randy's spirit.

We began the sessions with only five days of school left. I decided to skip the usual questions about the weather and so on and immediately asked: "Are you there?" I was surprised when the pointer moved quite rapidly toward yes, always a good sign. Instead of asking for a spelling of its name (which spirits frequently forget since names obviously have little meaning in the spirit world), I asked if it were Randy, and the pointer immediately went to yes.

Spirits are like people; in fact, I cannot emphasize enough that they *are* souls of people. Some were quite verbal during physical life and continue so in the spirit world; others, like Randy apparently, were not. Unlike some spirits who, in conjunction with the participants, have little difficulty helping to point to letters and spell out words, Randy generally seemed only able (willing?) to give yes and no answers. Asked if he had any message for Martha, he *did* manage to spell out "I love you," ending the first session rather emotionally.

Eventually during one of the sessions, I asked if he could flicker the fluorescent lights. The pointer immediately responded affirmatively. I asked if he would and nothing happened. I repeated both questions; the same responses followed. Had the students been moving the pointer, I thought they might have answered yes the second time. "You're not flickering the lights because you're restrained from doing so?" I asked, a point I hadn't discussed in class. The pointer immediately answered yes, hardly conclusive proof that spirits are restrained, I realize, but consistent with this book's findings.

Of course, the reliability of any similar information depends on the source, whether someone offers it here or in the spirit world. Certainly, information from intelligent, *verbal* spirits (like Arthur Ford or Seth) might be more accurate than from a laconic spirit like Randy. But this doesn't necessarily negate his contribution to the entire metaphysical picture, just as we wouldn't necessarily strike out a witness's testimony at a trial because we consider him generally less informed, less intelligent, or less articulate than another.

I hadn't discussed the "trapped spirit" idea and all of its ramifications with the class, so they lacked preconceived notions about it. Young people generally tend to be idealistic and more loving than older people. They frequently evaluate others optimistically, especially those close to their age like Randy. Therefore, when the next questions were answered negatively, I was fairly sure they weren't deliberately moving the pointer.

Randy wasn't happy where he was, he conveyed through a series of replies to questions, consistent with how trapped spirits respond about their situation. Asked if he were in heaven or hell, he responded negatively to both, also consistent. Since most of the class still maintained conventional attitudes about both, despite my discussions about different "areas" or "dimensions," I asked if he were therefore in purgatory. If the participants were deliberately moving the pointer, I would have expected yes, an obvious alternative unless Randy was playing with us, which I hadn't detected so far. Instead the pointer slid to no, surprising them because they had only deceived themselves into accepting the idea of other dimensions, just to please me and answer tests for good grades. I ended the experimenting there for the day, following it with another discussion about the idea of dimensions and trapped spirits.

WINDOW OF ETERNITY

We resumed the ouija board session the next day. Randy's overall attitude and consciousness immediately began looming negatively, consistent for trapped spirits. First he admitted being lonely. I pressed further, and he conveyed having difficulty "seeing" other spirits, logical since the chance of many or any spirits confining themselves to his small locale in the physical world instead of some area or dimension in the spirit world is slim.

In response to a series of questions, he conveyed feeling cold, surprising the class since I had mentioned that, lacking bodies, spirits generally lacked such feelings, although they could experience them if they thought they should, like Bill feeling cold beer traveling down the esophagus, for example.

Randy also indicated that he could see and hear us, consistent with other claims about the abilities of those who are conscious but out of the body. This also coincides with Dr. Moody's near-death patients who saw and heard doctors and others working over their bodies. In addition, Randy claimed he knew me, or at least remembered seeing me during his high school days.

Randy also indicated that up until then he hadn't realized that communication was possible via a ouija board and was enjoying it. We learned much about the spirit world and Christ from the questioning, supporting many of this book's theories. But the most interesting development occurred when I tried to counsel him.

"You realize, Randy, that waging war is wrong. If fact, all killing is wrong, especially taking another human's life, no matter what others say, including leaders of this or any other country." The pointer became immobile, and silence descended on the room, save for my voice.

"Don't you agree?" I pressed, and again, if the participants had been deliberately moving the pointer, they could have logically moved it to yes, consistent with their general idealism. That it remained motionless further convinced me that they were not. Once again they looked up at me, puzzled. But I was convinced, then, and am today, that I was getting through.

"You don't appreciate these questions about Vietnam, correct?" I asked, and the pointer never moved so quickly to yes.

"Randy, do you realize that you're dead, that you died in Vietnam?" I ventured, convinced he didn't. A yes would have surprised me, since most trapped spirits don't realize they're dead or that they're responsible for their own predicaments. A no would have been logical. But the pointer remained immobile again. Randy was more confused than I thought, I concluded.

"Randy, your physical life ended in Vietnam. Do you understand?" Not until I repeated several versions of this same point, for about five minutes, did the pointer finally begin moving slowly, as though begrudgingly, to yes.

Had the participants been purposely moving it, such deliberation, though logical and consistent with Randy's consciousness and situation, would have needed collusion and planning. Since the participants had no way of accurately anticipating my questions, how could they fake such a response?

Confident that Randy now accepted his physical death, I spent considerable time slowly and carefully explaining that physical death didn't end life and that the consciousness continued in the spirit world. "Do you understand?" I asked after every point, explaining further when it was necessary. Randy seemed like a child or like someone who had never carefully considered his physical actions before.

I had now paved the way for the next logical step concerning Randy, my ulterior motive for agreeing to use the ouija board. I began by telling him that he shouldn't be on earth because he was no longer a physical person but a spiritual entity and should reside in the spirit world where his relatives were undoubtedly waiting to greet him.

"In fact, your continuous attempts to manifest yourself in Martha's house are frightening Martha and her family," I continued, "and I'm sure that's not your intention, correct?" I asked. The pointer moved slowly toward yes amid dramatic silence. "Such manifestation serves no purpose since you no longer exist on earth nor can truly function adequately in physical form."

I embellished this speech, repeated it, and received Randy's affirmation that he now understood his situation. Except for some further questioning about other matters, this particular ouija board experiment ended. Looking back, I had used the ouija board for *constructive* reasons: out of kindness for Randy, in hopes of eliminating unnecessary alarm in Martha's family, and particularly to reinforce class discussions about such matters.

I had partically forgotten about the incident until the following year when I realized that Martha's sister Claire was in my class. Martha was now attending college and had recommended the course to Claire. One day when we were talking after class, Claire, apparently unaware of the ouija board experiment, mentioned that all unusual occurrences, including unprovoked footsteps and door-slamming, had finally ceased. The cessation happened at the same time that I had counseled Randy. He had apparently taken my advice and gone to the spirit world, I thought, smiling inwardly, and I briefly told Claire the whole story.

A spirit invariably becomes trapped on earth or wishes to reside here for any of many possible negative reasons, as I said before, but some can be positive. The pilot in the true story, *The Ghost of Flight 401*,[42] for example, continually struggled to physically manifest himself on earth (after dying in a crash) in order to warn others about some structural imperfections in a particular airplane his company had designed.

As I said earlier, most well-adjusted spirits are usually too preoccupied with spiritual matters to concern themselves with

---

[42]John Fuller, *The Ghost of Flight 401* (New York: Berkeley Publishing Corp., 1978).

us, even though they might think about and pray for us or send us love energy, depending on the individual spirit. Besides, they are just as much aware as we are that physical man must work out material problems himself. Of course, there is no set rule about how we should behave here or in the spirit world. We will always behave according to what we think is right at any given moment, although positive, constructive, or loving behavior always seems right or "good," unless improperly conceived or evaluated, no matter where performed, how or when. The problem is always finding the proper minds to evaluate it as such.

Though morally good spirits surely must appreciate good, physical people, direct intervention on their behalf on a large scale would not only be childish and unjust, preventing man from making certain changes and adjustments on his own as he proceeds to fulfill his own destiny, and would probably conflict with many just laws, causing chaos.

Dying violent or horrible deaths frequently causes earthly entrapment, as with Randy, especially for those ignorant about what follows physical death. Some spirits struggle to manifest themselves on earth out of jealousy for certain people, revenge, or because they cannot accept their unexpected, untimely deaths—all negative reasons. Maladjusted during physical life, they usually remain so afterwards unless they somehow develop new awareness about themselves.

A recent television documentary about physic phenomena described one such maladjusted spirit. A family moved into an old house somewhere in New England and began experiencing some highly unusual events. Something was causing an indentation on one of the children's beds, as though someone was sitting there when no one was. Other strange phenomena continued occurring until a parapsychologist was eventually contacted to communicate with what many, including the family, had concluded, was a ghost which they actually hadn't seen.

Upon arriving, the parapsychologist immediately detected

an "unseen presence" in the house, another example of individual differences in the spirit world, i. e., how some cannot fully materialize as ghosts, here. She began communicating with it, telephathically, learning that it had been a female (and still thought it was) during physical life. It was still living there, or struggling to, certainly contradicting what appears to be certain fundamental laws of the spirit world.

The story the parapsychologist learned about this female ghost is simple. Having lived in that very house centuries before, she had apparently reused to accept the news of her husband's death in a shipwreck. She herself died soon afterwards and remained in the house, brooding and highly confused as a trapped spirit, trying to function as though physically alive.

Unlike Randy, (assuming he followed my advice and truly entered the spirit world), this spirit refused to accept the parapsychologist's explanation that physical death had transpired, much less why it seemed bent on existing there. It completely ignored the parapsychologist's pleas to transcend to the spirit world, as if the parapsychologist was non-existent. It seemed completely lost, as though in shock, preoccupied only with a fixed thought—concern or deep fear about her husband, or simply waiting for him to return, a tragic situation. This spirit is comparable to stubborn, ignorant, or mentally sick people who simply refuse to listen to any other thoughts but their own. Unfortunately, she was probably still there and will remain there forever, unless she somehow begins to comprehend her situation and changes her attitude.

Chapter XI

The Power of the Subconscious

Most people generally scoff at the ouija board, closing their minds to its characteristics and peculiarities. They are convinced that the participants are deliberately moving the pointer, certainly true in some cases, although what such people might possibly gain from such fraud, save a few laughs and petty entertainment, is hard to imagine.

We all realize that the pointer cannot and does not propel itself, although cases have been reported where it has, indeed, shot out from underneath fingertips and landed some distance from the board. This is very rare, however, and depends on unusual circumstances and conditions. Such antics are frequently attributable to a playful or negative spirit or spirits.

Television, book, or movie portrayals of spirits literally able to unshelve and send books or heavier objects flying through the air during séances or ouija board sessions are simply far-fetched and absurd. Though I admit watching such supposed "supernatural" shows out of curiosity, I usually regret it. Unless they're based on strong, logical possibilities, such portrayals are usually negative, unrealistic, and frightening, and the less we expose our minds—our consciouses—to them, the better. It is imperative to recognize those dramatizations for what they are and not let such falsehoods influence us in any way.

Explanations abound concerning how or why the ouija pointer moves. Heat from the fingers is responsible, some claim, yet one participant apparently lacks enough heat to move it alone, and sometimes many participants can't move it either, suggesting unfavorable attitudes and/or conditions which can also affect a séance.

To illustrate, I tried using the ouija board again during the second year I taught "Perspective on Life and Death." One day the principal unexpectedly entered the room. His unfriendly intrusion had negative overtones. Though he had long since given me permission to teach the course, his attitude had apparently changed. The course had stimulated much interest and involvement, but I eventually learned that he was responding to a few parental complaints that our discussions were involving religion and the Bible. Anticipating such a reaction and realizing that teaching religion on the secondary level was against the law in my state, I had had the parents read and acknowledge a carefully worded letter detailing the course's subject matter beforehand, permitting their children to take the course. The principal too had read and approved the letter, but had forgotten all about it.

That day in class, the principal's disapproving presence seemed to affect the experiment immediately. When the pointer hardly moved at all for ten minutes, despite what I or anyone asked or said, I understood the meaning of an "unfavorable or inappropriate condition or situation." Oddly enough, here was a wonderful opportunity for students to impress their principal and prove the course's validity by deliberately moving the pointer, were they of that mind. Because they didn't doesn't necessarily prove that all good, intelligent students are honest, but that perhaps the majority of them are truly curious about seeking the truth.

The incredible peculiarity of the ouija board is that the inner self or the subconscious apprently moves the pointer. How else can we explain denials of deliberately moving it when it does, indeed, move? It cannot or does not normally move by itself, and those stubbornly insisting that someone consciously moves it, implying that every successful session must contain at least one liar, are narrow-minded, failing to consider an important alternative, possibly the only one.

Spirits don't generally move the pointer during a session or otherwise because they are restrained, as I have repeated; yet, apparently, they either communicate with or through one or more participants' consciouses or somehow directly influence the pointer's movement, a less likely explanation. The former is a very finite point, but so important it cannot be underestimated. For, if true, then spirits are constantly communicating with our subconsciouses or are capable of doing so under favorable conditions, providing we believe they can. Furthermore, it is through the subconscious that tuning in to the spirit world and/or God is possible, if desired, perhaps even automatic since ouija boards and the like are simply mediums.

Also, if all this is true, then praying directly to the superconscious is unnecessary or redundant because God (or the spirits) apparently know our deep-rooted, subconscious thoughts anyway. Besides, spirits in the spirit world probably receive these thoughts first, before the supposedly more advanced and developed superconscious. If anything, we probably should simply try sending love energy to those *here and* in the spirit world, as I have been maintaining, instead of repeatedly asking for God's help, favors or sympathy.

Just as the subconscious is capable of flip-flopping with the conscious during a ouija board session, the same supposedly occurs during "automatic writing" or "automatic typing" in Ruth Montgomery's case. In other words, if the individual can somehow completely preoccupy his conscious while sitting with pencil poised on a pad or fingers over keys, he can subconsciously write or type without conscious knowledge. Perhaps it is at this moment that spirits can communicate with or through us.

We all have the potential of achieving such conditions, but not all of us would ever want to. Some people are more successful participating with the ouija board or at a séance than at automatic writing. Others are afraid or think it's all nonsense, sinful, or devil-inspired. Deliberately changing awareness so that what we call "the subconscious" dominates the "conscious" isn't easy but possible and can frequently pave the way for interesting and highly controversial expeiences. An interesting reminder is that sleep is one particular deliberately-performed switch of the subconscious with the conscious which few of us would consider nonsense or sinful.

Critics might say that all instances of communication with spirits are hallucinations, or that information gathered during such contacts truly exists in some region of the person's mind or was obtained earlier.

To answer, it is practically common knowledge that hallucinations are mostly disjointed and illogical, and certainly not comparable to the detailed information provided by Arthur Ford, Robert Monroe, or Jane Roberts. That the latter could have subconsciously absorbed what amounts to many volumes of information years earlier, forgotten it, then effortlessly recited it during supposed trances assumes that she did some extensive and laborious "browsing" in earlier years.

If all knowledge about the spirit world is universally available, according to Plato, why have only Jane Roberts, Ruth Montgomery and a small percentage of the world population been able to learn it, rather than so-called intellectuals and other great minds of our times? Stress, preoccupation with false doctrines, close-mindedness, and low intelligence are among the major reasons why many of us are presently incapable of tapping into our subconsciouses and reaching such knowledge, though we have the potential of doing so, as evidenced by the handful who have.

It's far simpler and more logical to accept the idea that spirits such as Ford, Seth, and others have merely tried (and are still trying) to convey that the *spirit world does exist,* where they, Randy, and others reside, as we also shall one day.

Having supposedly contacted Randy's spirit during our classroom experiment, I recall that when someone else replaced Martha as a participant the pointer didn't move as well. Assuming she didn't deliberately move it, we can only conclude that she was somehow the catalyst for her Uncle Randy because their former relationship was close. Ruth Montgomery and Arthur Ford were good friends when Ford was alive, and Seth was supposedly close friends with the Robertses during their former reincarnations.

For some reason, contacting the spirit of a deceased person is easier from the particular house or building where the spirit once lived, died, or had a traumatic experience, since that is where it is probably existing as a trapped spirit.

Though many of us know of and accept telepathy, we're hardly trying to develop such powers although one day we might all communicate that way (as we do in the spirit world) because it's simple, quick, and inexpensive. But many others either hardly accept extrasensory preception or, if they do, merely store the concept in their mind without considering applying it. Concerted efforts to develop such abilities, undoubtedly inherent in all of us, probably won't start until or unless many individuals begin personally experiencing such "phenomena." Such new perception usually signals that the mind has taken or is ready for a new and exciting turn, whether or not it decides to take advantage of it. Most incredible (and just) is that we have undoubtedly been created so that we alone have the alternative of choosing to develop that way or not—an example of what I meant by being left alone to fulfill our own potentialities.

Consider the following personal ESP experience, or what psycholoists would call clairvoyance, exemplifying how we are capable of tuning into the inner self or of becoming consciously aware of subconscious information. One day, while meditating, I fell into a light sleep, or at least I thought so. As I awakened or, perhaps more accurately, as the subconscious began to recede, I clearly heard my grandson, then ten months old, making some unusually loud sounds. They were so vivid that I was convinced he was somewhere nearby in the house, until I remembered that he and his parents hadn't returned from a trip to town.

In fact, they didn't arrive until about two or three minutes later. After they entered the house, I immediately asked if the child had been making some unusually loud sounds just before. Both were surprised, admitting that he had suddenly and unexpectantly done so just a few miles from the house, although he had been quiet before and since. I could not have consciously heard him over such a distance, especially since it was winter and car and house windows were closed.

Another example of "tapping" into the subconscious occurred that summer. One day I hired two teen-agers to help me cut firewood for my fireplace. One of them had received permission to cut wood on his uncle's land. Pulling a fairly heavy trailer and driving along the highway, I had been following his directions without any problem until he told me to make a particular right onto a dirt road about a half-mile ahead. Something strange happened in my mind the moment he spoke, as though I had suddenly received a strong impulse from the subconscious. Though I hadn't questioned his directions all along, I recall becoming extremely nervous and irritable while slowing down. "Are you sure?" I practically demanded. He answered that he was. "The next right?" I kept repeating.

"Yes, I'm positive," he insisted. I suddenly experienced a tremendous urge not to cut wood that day, much less turn right. In fact, I pulled over before the turn, stopped, and refused to go on. Only after he continued to insist that we were at the right place (as all of us inspected about as much of the road as was observable before it leveled off, curving out of sight into thick woods), did I finally venture down, but very reluctantly, though it appeared safe. As soon as I did, and we arrived at the turn, I was forced to stop, amazed. Ahead was a huge mound of earth, a roadblock, purposely bulldozed to block trespassers. This, indeed, was the wrong turn, and we should have taken the next one, we eventually learned.

Because of heavy vegetation lining both sides of the road, we could only drive backwards, almost impossible because the gravel was slippery and I couldn't develop enough speed on such an incline. In fact, we first had to unhook and push out the trailer, which the three of us barely managed, and then, because of spinning wheels, the boys had to push the car while I backed out.

I had apparently tried to warn myself (precognition) of imminent danger or an impending mistake which could have proven more disastrous than all of us simply wasting several hours and plenty of energy, ending wood cutting for that day. We could have been arrested for trespassing, and I could have gotten stuck, requiring a wrecker. Oddly enough, my wife, who is frequently psychic, had warned me against going there although possibly only because she was always less trusting of teen-age responsibility than I.

I have had similar ESP experiences and warnings since then (though less frequently) and have tried to pay more attention to them. The point is perfectly clear — that some aspect of the brain, call it the subconscious or inner self, probably has more potential insight and awareness than we realize. In fact, the subconscious is either all-knowing or has the ability to acquire more knowledge, insight, or truth than we ever thought possible. Unfortunately, too many of us today are too preoccupied with all that's material and even physical to be in touch with our subconscious. Lacking modern conveniences and gadgetry, early man was certainly more reflective and spiritual than modern man and probably more attuned to ESP. He lived closer to the land and very little distracted him. Such people contemplated more and were probably more able to reach their inner selves, at least more frequently than modern man.

But blaming modern civilization for our worldly, unspiritual attitudes, or completely rejecting society is illogical, unrealistic, and perhaps even unfair to the self. It's impossible to fully develop our potentialities of the self or even to perfect the self and eliminate faults unless we become involved with man and civilization. In fact, perhaps our superconsciousness could not fully realize its own potential unless or until it created the physical world and man, and suffered all the agonies and frustrations watching him progress or destroy himself. Living (and/or suffering) in a rat race can teach us much, providing we can overcome the stresses and anxieties it creates and not become slaves to its many evils and false sense of values. The more we face and recognize what men are in particular environments, the more we can keep such behavior, as bad as it might be, in proper perspective since we're all evolving, spiritually and morally, and possibly begin to change it. The more people reject such environments, the less such evil environments will exist and flourish.

To reiterate, those maintaining that mediums are too simple, have been around too long, and couldn't possibly be the key to communicatin with spirits or the superconsciousness miss the point. *We* make such penetration possible — more precisely, our subconscious minds do, not mediums. Remember, the Robertses innocently began with the ouija board, then discontinued when Jane Roberts began communicating directly with Seth through, by means of, or in conjunction with her subconscious, the real vehicle here. What is most important, however, is realizing how reaching the subconscious can *help us function better in this and the next world.* It can make us more aware of ourselves, others, the spirit world, and our creator. But only through meditation can we clear away enough anxiety and stressful debris to catch those subtle glimpses of the past, future, and aspects of the spirit world that invariably spring from the subconscious.

Chapter XII

Purpose and Reincarnation

I've delayed analyzing the question concerning what our purpose is in life because the subject is complex, highly controversial, and first requires some background information.

Throughout history, people have asked themselves and others what their purpose is other than simply to live out each day for about seventy years and then pass away. I have difficulty speculating about my own purpose (although I believe I understand parts of it), much less anyone else's and certainly the more difficult creator's. Certainly we appear to have many lesser purposes in physical life than perfecting our souls, the general one. Certain theories seem clear, which I shall reveal in hopes that others might accept and apply them, aiding in understanding themselves and their roles in life.

I spent perhaps two or three years avoiding even the slightest consideration of reincarnation, possibly out of general stubbornness, my own previous religious background, or simply because reincarnation was too foreign for me as a Westerner. Struggling to understand the meaning of life, I kept getting nowhere, running into mental dead ends. Yet I refused to accept the idea that life was truly purposeless, which seemed too negative, absurd, and inconsistent with the creator's supposed love. Once I finally began to accept the possibility of reincarnation, the pieces began fitting together logically.

Spiritual existence probably preceded and later created the physical universe and physical life, especially since the superconsciousness or the forces comprising it seem to be spiritual and because that seems to be our final, eternal existence. That our superconsciousness might be physical would imply that it either exists in our physical universe (and can ultimately be reached or contacted physically) or exists in another physical dimension.

Again, it is simpler to accept what is less complicated and far more logical—that the creator was, is, and probably will be spiritual, though certainly capable of creating physical and other manifestations of itself, particularly man and other physical creatures throughout the universe. Trying to determine who or what created our particular superconsciousness, however, is futile and perhaps unknowable until we return to the spirit world. The moment we claim that our superconsciousness came from or was created by another superconsciousness, we immediately want to know who or what created that superconsciousness, and so on, ad infinitum. It is easier simply to accept the existence of our superconsciousness and proceed from there.

Logically, then, our superconsciousness created spirits like you and me, or perhaps we broke away from it, or are some kind of manifestation or aspect of it, however one wishes to describe our separation from the superconsciousness. In fact, our subconsciouses undoubtedly know precisely how or what happened and possess other answers about God, the universe, and the spirit world, if only we could gain easy access to that domain. In any case, we all possess separate awareness and chose, or in some way the creator directed us, to reside in a physical body in order to seek perfection, purification, become greater than we are or know more.

Whether or not new spirits are still breaking from our superconsciousness, a question many students ask, is difficult to determine. Probably they are not, since they wouldn't have accumulated enough general information from previous reincarnations (stored in the subconscious) to help them adjust to our civilization quickly and easily. Most of us have probably reincarnated several times, explaining how and why early learning and adjustment are relatively easy.

Since we already know that men have been and still are quite morally and physically imperfect, the question arises: why weren't our spirits created more perfectly or in a more advanced stage so that, reincarnated into physical man, we wouldn't have had to suffer so much physical and mental pain? The question is difficult to answer, but, left with man's undeniable nature, we can speculate.

As discussed earlier, I reject the idea of the creator purposely creating an extremely evil spirit, Satan, who, in the form of a snake, ultimately tempts Adam and Eve into sinning. This seems too unfair, negative, and even silly. Nor can I accept original sin, redemption, and that entire, very complicated arrangement.

Throughout this book I have suggested another reason for our present arrangement. Collectively, we probably represent some underdeveloped, undesirable, imperfect or even evil aspect of the superconsciousness that cannot be cleansed, erased, improved, or perfected by any other means other than through many physical reincarnations, each spirit working out its individual tasks and problems, separately, in physical bodies. Why the superconsciousness must, or elected to operate this way, if indeed it did (does), is hard to determine since it is difficult or perhaps impossible to understand the details of its existence and its purposes until our consciouses are developed enough to do so, here or in the spirit world.

Physical man's fate is such that many of us must suffer in this process of development, and certainly those struggling to be morally good in a sea of many morally imperfect or evil creatures probably suffer more than others, although suffering is relative to the nature of each individual spirit and the purposes and goals he arranges for himself. Physical life *does* also offer many happy, fulfilling moments, even years, for some, once again depending on that soul's characteristics, what it wishes to accomplish on earth, and other complex variables including what it did or did not accomplish in former lives.

But the point is that we probably learn best and more thoroughly through suffering which, I suppose, is unfortunate but peculiar to our nature and reality. Suffering perfects us, as it probably does our creator. Having created us, it is deeply involved with us. Perceiving our suffering, it undoubtedly suffers on a proportion beyond our comprehension, if that's any consolation, particularly because it saw no other alternative out of its own dilemma than to permit such offering.

If the reader still rejects this suffering angle, consider it another way. The creator wouldn't have been stupid or unkind enough to allow us to suffer unless there was no other way it could accomplish what it wishes to accomplish. Instead of complaining about occasional suffering throughout our lives (much of which we cause ourselves, incidentally), we should accept our fate and be happy that we've been included in the creator's design and have been given a separate existence. Hopefully, through continual reincarnations, man will become a greater, more perfected creature, and will eventually suffer less, centuries hence, along with our creator.

Since few of us are morally and physically perfect now, reincarnation will probably continue for a long time, until or unless man destroys himself beforehand. In fact, even if man perfects himself to the point that war, murder, and other evils become obsolete by the year 2,500, say, reincarnation will probably continue until total perfection is achieved, or until all men become completely tuned in, until all will know, will be harmoniously and consistent with the whole and will have achieved complete oneness with the creator, most likely eons from now.

If and when such perfection is achieved, perhaps man will become completely transformed into spirit form (as Christ might have been when he supposedly reappeared on earth following physical death) or simply remain spiritual in the spirit world and not need to reincarnate. No longer needing the physical universe, such spiritual forces might cause the physical universe to collapse and cease, only to explode and start the process again somewhere else in another moment of our superconsciousness's time and dimension, using itself or another aspect of itself as the source.

After returning to the spirit world following physical death, spirits invariably contemplate how much they developed in the last incarnation and usually try again (reincarnate) since perfection is rarely achieved in all areas. A spirit could possibly choose to wait for centuries to reincarnate or might simply await the proper parents or other conditions such as the necessary moral environment.

Having reached a certain developmental level, it could even choose never to reincarnate. It could remain in a dimension containing comparably advanced spirits—a kind of heaven—where Jesus, Buddha, and other great spirits possibly reside. Or, if sufficiently advanced, a spirit could even join the superconsciousness in order to further enhance it. Such an area of existence isn't pure imagination or wishful thinking, since many near-death patients have perceived entire "cities" (dimensions) containing indescribably glorious beings.

That we weren't created capable of remembering one or more former lives, so that we could analyze and correct past mistakes, might seem illogical or unfair at first. But such awareness would probably create more havoc and complications than it would help. First would be the problem of trying to block out or forget images of relationships with former parents, relatives, friends, and other loved ones so they wouldn't interfere with new ones. Also, unable to walk or perform other "remembered" physical tasks and skills, we probably would become unnecessarily frustrated in the limited vehicle of a baby's body for such a long time. And remembering former lives, reincarnated spirits might be too tempted to seek out and punish those, still alive, who gave them grief, hurt, or even killed them in their previous life or lives.

Likewise, fearing some form of revenge or retribution, or anticipating an uncomfortable situation, we might suddenly begin refusing even to reincarnate at all, defeating its main purpose, possibly slowing or ending man's general development. In addition, imagine the complicated personal problems facing us upon realizing, say, that our present mother was actually a former wife, sister, or even father in a previous existence? What about the guilt and horror we would suffer remembering that we killed someone in a former life?

Still, some might argue that if reincarnation is the answer to physical life, why can't we remember at least something from a former life? First of all, many of us can barely remember incidents from our early childhood, much less details. How can we expect to remember events that possibly occurred hundreds of years before during former lives? Some of us have "unexplained" glimpses of events, never realizing they are really from a past life. Sometimes they occur during the day and are disregarded or blamed on something else, and sometimes they occur during dreams and are thus considered simply part of the dreams.

That some of us *are* capable of analyzing one or more former lives under hypnosis (regression) might seem contradictory. But remember, such information is hardly accessible, and we were undoubtedly created (or have developed in such a way as) to have difficulty obtaining it because of its probable negative and uncomplimentary nature. Besides, not everyone is capable of being hypnotized or would want to be, much less be regressed to a former life which they might fear.

It is true that the morally good always suffer because of or at the hands of the morally bad. But far more importantly, remember that life undoubtedly continues after physical death. Therefore, physical life isn't as important or as vital and "real" as we think. What *is* vital however is to remember that we are *not* totally helpless in this scheme of things. We can and will progress morally and spiritually when we are truly prepared to recognize what we have been, still are, and might be destined to become. We must see our faults clearly and make a sincere effort to change them.

As we change our own consciousness and become more loving, giving and sincere, we will not only prepare ourselves better for the next world, but will in a real way help change the consciousness of *this* world and make it a better place.

BIBLIOGRAPHY

Bernstein, Morey. *The Search for Birdie Murphy.* Garden City, New York: Doubleday and Co., 1956.
Bloomfield, Harold, M.D. *Transcendental Meditation.* New York: Dell Publication Co., 1975.
Castaneda, Carlos. *Journey to Ixtlan.* New York: Simon and Schuster, 1973
Castaneda, Carlos. *The Teachings of Don Juan.* New York: Ballentine Books, 1969.
Evans-Wentz, W. Y., ed. *The Tibetan Book of the Dead.* New York: Oxford University Press, 1957.
Fuller, John. *The Ghost of Flight 401.* New York: Berkley Publishing Corp., 1978.
Hanford, James H., ed. *The Poems of John Milton.* New York: The Ronald Press Company, 1953.
Head, L. and Cranston, S. L. *Reincarnation: The Phoenix Fire Mystery.* New York: Julian Press/Crown Publishers, Inc., 1977.
Herrigel, Eugen. *The Method of Zen.* New York: Vintage Books, 1974.
Herrigel, Eugen. *Zen in the Art of Archery.* New York: Random House, 1971.
Jacobson, Nils O., M. D. *Life Without Death.* New York: Dell Publishing Co., 1973.
Klein, Aaron E. and Cynthia. *Mind Trips.* New York: Doubleday, 1979.
Kubler-Ross, Elisabeth. *On Death and Dying.* New York: Macmillan, 1969.
Monroe, James. *Journeys Out of the Body.* New York: Anchor Press, 1977.
Montgomery, Ruth. *A World Beyond.* New York: Coward, Mc Cann, and Geoghegan, 1971.
Moody, Raymond A., M. D. *Life After Life.* New York: Bantam Books, Inc., 1976.
Moody, Raymond A., M. D. *Reflections on Life After Life.* New York: Bantam Books, Inc., 1978.
Pearce, Joseph C. *The Crack in the Cosmic Egg.* New York: Pocket Books, 1973.
Rawlings, Maurice, M. D. *Beyond Death's Door.* Nashville: Thomas Nelson Inc., Publishers, 1978.
Ritchie, George. *Return from Tomorrow.* Lincoln, Virginia: Chosen Books, 1977.
Roberts, Jane. *How to Develop ESP Power.* New York: Frederick Fell, 1966.
Roberts, Jane. *The Seth Material.* Englewood Cliffs, New Jersey: Prentice-Hall, Inc., 1970.
Roberts, Jane. *Seth Speaks.* Englewood Cliffs, New Jersey: Prentice-Hall, Inc., 1972.
Sagan, Carl. *The Cosmos.* New York: Random House, 1980.
Smith, T. V. *Philosophers Speak for Themselves.* Chicago, Illinois: The University of Chicago Press, 1952.
Steiner, Rudolf. *Knowledge of the Higher Worlds.* London: Rudolf Steiner Press, 1969.

Wambach, Helen. *Life Before Life.* New York: Bantam Books, Inc., 1979.
Way, The (The Living Bible). Wheaton, Illinois: Tyndale House Publishers, 1972.
Weiss, Jess E. *The Vestibule.* Port Washington, New York: Ashley Books, 1972.
Welch, Thomas. *Oregon's Amazing Miracle.* Dallas: Christ for the Nations, Inc., 1976.
World Book Encyclopedia, The 22 vols. Chicago: Field Enterprise Corp., 1974.